THE VISITOR'S GUIDE TO
AMERICAN
GARDENS

Garden **Walks**	Garden **Talks**	Garden **Events**

First published in 2011 by Cool Springs Press, an imprint of the Quayside Publishing Group, P.O. Box 2828, Brentwood, TN 37024 USA.

Cool Springs Press titles are also available at discounts in bulk quantity for industrial or sales-promotional use. For details write to Special Sales Manager at Cool Springs Press, P.O. Box 2828, Brentwood, TN 37024 USA.

To find out more about our books, visit us online at www.coolspringspress.com.

ISBN-13: 978-1-59186-527-8

Library of Congress Cataloging-in-Publication Data

Sharp, Jo Ellen Meyers.
 The visitor's guide to American gardens, garden walks, garden talks & garden events / Jo Ellen Meyers Sharp.
   p. cm.
 ISBN 978-1-59186-527-8 (pbk. : alk. paper)
1. Gardens--United States--Guidebooks. 2. Botanical gardens--United States--Guidebooks. 3. Arboretums--United States--Guidebooks. 4. Gardens--Canada--Guidebooks. 5. Botanical gardens--Canada--Guidebooks. 6. Arboretums--Canada--Guidebooks. I. Title.

 SB466.U6S49 2011
 580'.73--dc23

                              2011029250

President/CEO: Ken Fund
Group Publisher: Bryan Trandem
Publisher: Ray Wolf
Senior Editor: Billie Brownell
Editor: Kathy Franz
Creative Director: Michele Lanci
Design: Bill Kersey
Production Manager: Hollie Kilroy
Photo Researcher: Krystyna Borgen
Production: S.E. Anderson

Printed in the United States of America

10 9 8 7 6 5 4 3 2 1

THE VISITOR'S GUIDE TO
AMERICAN
GARDENS

Garden **Walks**   Garden **Talks**   Garden **Events**

Jo Ellen Meyers Sharp

COOL
SPRINGS
PRESS

Growing Successful Gardeners™

BRENTWOOD, TENNESSEE

Photography Credits

Cool Springs Press extends its thanks to the staff of all
the botanical gardens and parks whose profiles appear in this book.
In particular, we wish to thank them for the use of their images.
We hope that you, the reader, will have the opportunity to visit each one!

TABLE OF CONTENTS

Acknowledgments 7

Dedication 7

Introduction 8

How to Use This Book 10

Botanical Garden Profiles 14

Garden Walks, Garden Talks & Garden Events 297

Major Garden Events and Tours of England,
Europe, and Other Parts of the World 308

State & Regional Maps 310

Meet Jo Ellen Meyers Sharp 336

Acknowledgments

With thanks to Cool Springs Press for allowing me to be a part of this new guide for touring gardens, to Billie Brownell and Kathy Franz for their editing skills, and to Krystyna Borgen for photo selections. I'd also like to thank Cindy Games, former publisher of Cool Springs Press, for her encouragement and support.

Most important, I'm grateful to the late Roger Waynick, founder of Cool Springs Press, for the tremendous opportunity he gave me and for his legacy in the world of gardening communications. Thanks, too, to Garden Writers Association, whose meetings have allowed me to visit so many of these beautiful places firsthand.

Jo Ellen

> ## Dedicated
> *to gardeners who seek beauty in their travels.*

Introduction

I am an inveterate traveler, and I've been privileged to visit some spectacular gardens. What a treat it's been. Because you have this book, I know you are a fellow garden tourist. Or maybe you are new to garden tourism—in that case, welcome!

When garden tourists travel, we pack our walking shoes, camera, notepad (paper or electronic), pen, and our life list of gardens. For many of us, we don't even have to leave our community, certainly not our state or province, to see beautifully designed landscapes and to-die-for plant combinations. This book helps you explore these earthy adventures at home and away.

Some states, such as California, New York, and Florida, are rich with gardens, from the gaudy to the glorious. Pennsylvania claims the home and garden of John Bartram, considered America's first horticulturist. In Virginia, George Washington's Mount Vernon and Thomas Jefferson's Monticello remain testaments to our early presidents' love of gardens for food and pleasure.

For some of us, the beauty is as close as our city park or a nearby historic mansion and landscape. The Olmsted Brothers firm in Massachusetts not only designed Central Park in New York City, but also the park systems in Boston, Louisville, and many other cities and towns. Olmsted also designed the residential landscapes of well-to-do industrialists, including the Biltmore Estate in North Carolina. George Kessler, another urban planning pioneer, designed city parks throughout the Midwest and South, including locations in Indianapolis, Kansas City, Memphis, and Dallas. Jens Jensen, a contemporary of Frank Lloyd Wright, fostered a prairie style that celebrated Midwestern sensibilities with fine examples throughout the Chicago park district and elsewhere.

Personally, I've visited many of the gardens in this guide. One of my favorites is Chanticleer in Wayne, Pennsylvania, known as a "pleasure garden," which indeed it is. Its history is less important than the ambience of Chanticleer, where tropicals surround the residence, sculpture adorns the grounds, and pathways reveal surprises at each turn, including the playful use of plants. Where else would you find tobacco grown as an ornamental plant, appreciated for its flower and size?

Another delight is the Madoo Conservancy in Sagaponack, New York, a two-acre speck on Long Island that serves as the home and studio of artist Robert Dash. Here, visitors walk through doors in the landscape, climb stairs for a bird's-eye view, and relax to the sound of calming fountains.

Manitou Park in Spokane is a green relief to the steppe topography that defines western Washington. Near Vancouver is the delightful Minter Garden, where eye-popping color, heavily planted beds, and a wall of water delight the senses.

I would be remiss if I did not name the beautiful Indianapolis Museum of Art and its historic Oldfields House and Gardens in my introduction (after all, Indianapolis is my hometown). The meticulously restored garden and home recall another time, when wealthy Americans retreated to their country estates for summers and holidays. But the other gardens, including the new Virginia B. Fairbanks Art & Nature Park, known locally as 100 Acres, offer beautiful examples of mature plantings that foster an appreciation for outdoor beauty year-round.

These and other gardens entertain us, soothe us, inspire us, and restore us. When we visit them, we gain an appreciation of the fine work of Mother Nature and of man, and we learn how we can incorporate many of these attributes in our own gardens and our own style.

Now, let's get on the road!

How to Use This Book

With this book, we've pulled together all the basic information that you need to visit gardens throughout the United States and Canada. Like a good companion, we guide your journey by highlighting what certain gardens are known for, such as a rose or daylily collection, historic significance, children's activities, or art in the landscape.

Information about the gardens came from websites, personal visits, correspondence, and the reviews, comments, and recommendations from colleagues. We've tried to be as inclusive as possible, but that said, we're sure we've overlooked some gardens that warrant inclusion. We hope you will drop us a note with your suggestions or comments.

To enhance your visit to gardens, in the back of this book we've listed other horticultural or nature-related activities in the community, such as tours of private gardens, family programs, outdoor exhibits, or concerts.

TIPS ON VISITING GARDENS

There are a few things visitors can do to make sure their visits to gardens are as enjoyable as possible. Feel free to make notes or take photos of plant combinations or arrangements that you like and can use in your own landscape. Here are some tips:

- **Wear comfortable shoes.** Many paths, especially in arboretums or natural areas, are covered with gravel or wood chips. Some trails may be steep and require firm footing to make the trek. If there's rain, some paths will get wet, muddy, and slippery.
- **Anticipate the weather and dress appropriately.** In some climates during some seasons, the weather can change quickly, causing temperatures to drop within a few hours. Pack an umbrella or rain gear and carry a jacket. Wear sunscreen and use insect repellents, if necessary.
- **Think green.** Take out what you take in. Some gardens do not allow food on the grounds or they ask that you not leave trash. Some have picnic areas. Always dispose of trash in appropriate containers.
- **Stay on the pathways.** Do not walk in the garden beds.
- **Call ahead.** Most gardens allow visitors to take photos and videos for their own personal use. However, many do not allow tripods. Professional and commercial photographers are asked to check with a garden's office for information on permission forms, fees, or restrictions.
- **Do not pick anything.** At all but a few gardens, visitors are not allowed to remove plants, seeds, or cuttings.
- **Allow enough time to enjoy the gardens.** Remember that gardens are for strolling and set a pace by their curves, vistas, or plant arrangements. Don't forget to smell the roses.

ICONS

The Visitor's Guide to American Gardens uses icons to indicate certain amenities.

 Indicates there is food service on-site other than vending machines. Hours of service may be different from garden hours and days of operation.

 Some gardens are fully ADA accessible while others have limited accessibility. Some, such as historic homes, may be wheelchair accessible on the first floor only. Gardens or arboretums sometimes have paved and gravel pathways and some may be steep. Some gardens also provide audio and visual materials. Most gardens suggest contacting their office before visiting to ensure all your needs can be met.

 Indicates a special collection of plants, such as a rose garden or conifers.

 Indicates there's a children's garden or other activity designed to entertain or interest kids.

 Shows where gardens may have fountains or other water features, or views of water, such as a lake, river, or ocean.

 Specifies a historic property, usually listed on the National Register of Historic Places or a similar state or county significance.

 Shows where there are regular annual events, such as plant sales, seminars, workshops, concerts, or exhibits, usually too many to list in this guide. We recommend checking a garden's website to see what's going on before visiting.

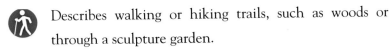 Describes walking or hiking trails, such as woods or through a sculpture garden.

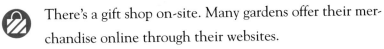 There's a gift shop on-site. Many gardens offer their merchandise online through their websites.

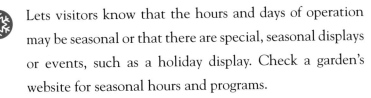 Lets visitors know that the hours and days of operation may be seasonal or that there are special, seasonal displays or events, such as a holiday display. Check a garden's website for seasonal hours and programs.

WHAT'S WITH THIS FUNNY BOX?

That's what's called a "QR" code (an abbreviation for "Quick Response"). They are images that can be scanned by your smartphone's camera to link to the websites of our featured gardens. We also made a special QR code— the one to the right—that will take you to a webpage of information and directions for *all* of the gardens listed in this guide.

You'll need to have a QR code reader on your smartphone or mobile device. If you don't already have one, they're easy to find and usually free to download. Search for "QR Code reader" in your device's app store, or check online.

You will find QR codes used throughout *The Visitor's Guide to American Gardens*. We hope you will use this feature to visit the gardens' websites, take a virtual tour, use a GPS device, discover additional gardens, and much more.

Bellingrath Gardens & Home

Address 12401 Bellingrath Gardens Rd., Theodore, 36582
Phone (800) 247-8420
Website www.bellingrath.org
Hours Year-round, 8 a.m. to 5 p.m.
Fee Yes, varies according to tour selection

The museum-home and gardens sit on 900 acres along the Fowl River. Built by an early Coca-Cola bottler in Mobile, Bellingrath has been open to the public since the 1930s. Planted on the 65 cultivated acres are camellias, hydrangeas, lilies, delphiniums, caladiums, mums, and other native and tropical plants. In spring, 250,000 azaleas explode with color. With 2,000 roses planted in large blocks of color, the All-America Rose Selections named Bellingrath a Top Public Rose Garden in 2004.

Birmingham Botanical Garden

Address 2612 Lane Park Rd., Birmingham, 35223
Phone (205) 414-3950
Website www.bbgardens.org
Hours Dawn to dusk
Fee No

There are more than two dozen separate garden areas on the 69-acre Birmingham Botanical Garden, including a crape myrtle garden, camellia house, fern glade, iris garden, Southern Living Garden, hosta walk, herb terrace, and enabling garden. The Japanese Gardens have an authentic teahouse, and the wildflower garden holds more than 400 species native to Alabama and includes a 7-acre rock garden. The Forman Garden is the perfect scale for homeowners to interpret ideas for their landscapes.

Aldridge Botanical Gardens

Address 3530 Lorna Rd., Hoover, 35216
  Phone (205) 682-8019
Website www.aldridgegardens.com
   Hours Nov. 1–Mar. 15, 8 a.m. to 5 p.m.; Mar. 15–Apr. 30, 8 a.m. to 7 p.m.;
           May 1–Sept. 14, 8 a.m. to 8 p.m.; Sept. 15–Oct. 31, 8 a.m. to 7 p.m.
     Fee No

This 30-acre woodland garden was the home of Eddie Aldridge, who discovered the native oakleaf hydrangea called 'Snowflake', which is planted throughout. The property includes a walking trail, birding opportunities, and a 6-acre lake. Open since 2002, the garden is owned by the City of Hoover.

Huntsville Botanical Garden

Address 4747 Bob Wallace Ave., Huntsville, 35805
  Phone (256) 830-4447
Website www.hsvbg.org
   Hours Apr.–Sept., Monday–Saturday, 9 a.m. to 6 p.m., Thursday, 9 a.m. to 8 p.m.,
           Sunday, noon to 6 p.m.; Oct.–Mar., Monday–Saturday, 9 a.m. to 5 p.m.,
           Sunday, noon to 5 p.m.
     Fee Yes, winter discount Dec.–Feb.

More than 13 distinct gardens fill the 112-acre Huntsville Botanical Garden, including a Biblical garden, perennial and annual borders featuring plants that do well in the Southern garden, daylilies, herbs, a butterfly garden, and dogwoods. A 2-acre children's garden and a trail through native lowland forest are also noteworthy.

Mobile Botanical Garden

Address 5151 Museum Dr., Mobile, 36608
Phone (251) 342-0555
Website www.mobilebotanicalgardens.org
Hours Dawn to dusk
Fee No

The Mobile Botanical Garden has one of the most comprehensive collections of rhododendrons and azaleas in the South, with more than 1,000 of the shrubs planted. It also has a collection of Japanese maples, ferns, camellias, and a preserved habitat of longleaf pines on the garden's 100 acres.

Jasmine Hill Garden and Outdoor Museum

Address 3001 Jasmine Hill Rd., Montgomery, 36106
Phone (334) 567-6463
Website www.jasminehill.org
Hours July–Oct., Saturdays, 9 a.m. to 5 p.m.
Fee Yes

Known as a "little corner of Greece" built in the outcroppings of the Appalachian Mountains, at least 40 pieces of reproduction and original Greek and Roman art fill the 20-acre garden, which contains hundreds of seasonal ornamental plants, including many winter varieties.

Alaska Botanical Garden

Address 4601 Campbell Airstrip Rd., Anchorage, 99520
Phone (907) 770-3692
Website www.alaskabg.org
Hours Daylight hours year-round
Fee Yes

Chance glimpses of moose and bear amid boreal spruce and birch forests are an added attraction in this 110-acre garden that features hiking, birding, and photogenic views of the Chugach Mountain Range. Specialty gardens include herbs and a rock garden with 350 alpine plants. More than 1,100 species of perennials and 150 native plants provide living examples of sub-arctic gardening through the growing season and winter. The new East Garden is home to a Gold Medal Peony Collection.

Georgeson Botanical Garden

Address 117 W. Tanana Dr., Fairbanks, 99775
Phone (907) 474-7222
Website www.georgesonbg.org
Hours May–Sept., 9 a.m. to 8 p.m. daily
Fee Yes

As part of the University of Alaska Fairbanks, the Georgeson Botanical Garden is a prime testing site for 300 annuals and several hardy roses along with thousands of trees, shrubs, and perennials. It also is one of five test gardens for the International Hardy Fern Foundation.

Jensen-Olson Arboretum

Address 23035 Glacier Hwy., Juneau, 99801
Phone (907) 789-0139
Website www.juneau.org/parkrec/arboretum-main.php
Hours Year-round, Wednesday–Sunday, 9 a.m. to 5 p.m.
Fee No

Seasonal flowerbeds and spectacular views of the Chilkat Mountains and a vegetable garden that's been in existence for more than 100 years are highlights of the arboretum at Pearl Harbor on Favorite Channel. The garden belonged to Master Gardener Caroline Jensen, who donated it to the city.

Arizona-Sonora Desert Museum

Address 2021 N. Kinney Rd., Tucson, 85743
Phone (520) 883-2702
Website www.desertmuseum.org
Hours Year-round, daily
Fee Yes

The Arizona-Sonora Desert Museum includes a zoo, botanical garden, art institute, and natural history museum on 98 acres. This location has one of the finest collections of animals and insects indigenous to the desert and is considered a pioneer in how animals are displayed in their natural habitats. More than 40,000 plants are maintained on the grounds. To illustrate the inter-relationships, geologic specimens and concepts are incorporated into the exhibits. Fossil and vertebrate paleontology collections contain the skeleton of a dinosaur found in Arizona.

Desert Botanical Garden

Address 1201 N. Galvin Parkway, Phoenix, 85008
Phone (480) 941-1225
Website www.dbg.org
Hours 7 a.m. to 8 p.m. daily
Fee Yes

More than 4,000 species of desert plants fill 65 of the Desert Botanical Garden's 145 acres. In 2010, the garden's agave and cactus families were designated National Collections by the American Public Gardens Association. The Plants and People of the Sonoran Desert Trail takes visitors through five demonstration habitats that explain how they have been used for food, fiber, medicine, or cultural interest for 2,000 years. A highlight of the garden is the Chihuly Desert Towers, which were created especially for the garden, and which stand at the entrance.

Arboretum at Flagstaff

Address 4001 S. Woody Mountain Rd., Flagstaff, 86001
Phone (928) 774-1442
Website www.thearb.org
Hours Apr. 1–Oct. 31, 9 a.m. to 5 p.m.
Fee Yes

This 200-acre arboretum, 7,000 feet above sea level, represents the high-desert Colorado Plateau, which is also home to the Grand Canyon and Zion National Park. More than 2,500 native plants that represent this region are planted throughout the arboretum. The arboretum also houses the Merriam-Powell Research Station.

Tucson Botanical Garden

Address 2150 N. Alvernon Way, Tucson, 85712
Phone (520) 326-9686
Website www.tucsonbotanical.org
Hours 8:30 a.m. to 4:30 p.m. daily
Fee Yes

Look for education kits throughout the garden; these are interactive touch carts that allow visitors to learn more about the desert and its plant and animal inhabitants. A Garden Railway opened recently, complete with a miniature train town. Other gardens are designed to showcase birding, wildflowers, and overall enjoyment.

Garvan Woodland Gardens

Address 550 Arkridge Rd., Hot Springs National Park, 71913
Phone (800) 366-4664
Website www.garvangardens.com
Hours 9 a.m. to 6 p.m. daily
Fee Yes

The Garvan Woodland Gardens feature hundreds of rare shrubs and trees, including camellias, magnolias, and more than 160 different types of azaleas. Many antique roses grace the Border of Old Roses. Japanese maples and tree peonies serve as an introduction to the Japanese-inspired Garden of the Pine Wind. Rock gardens, a conifer border, and a growing number of bulbs and perennials complete the collection, providing interest throughout the year. The garden is part of the University of Arkansas School of Architecture.

Botanical Garden of the Ozarks

Address 4703 N. Crossover Rd., Fayetteville, 72764
Phone (479) 750-2620
Website www.bgozarks.org
Hours 9 a.m. to 5 p.m. daily
Fee Yes

Besides an Ozark native plant garden, this 86-acre site includes specialty gardens such as children's and four-season gardens, sensory and Japanese gardens, rose and perennial gardens, and water, rock, and food gardens. Other highlights include the Carl A. Totemeier Horticulture Center. A bat tower was built to protect the endangered Ozark big-eared bat.

Eureka Springs Gardens

Address 1537 CR 201, Eureka Springs, 72632
Phone (479) 253-9244
Website www.bluespringheritage.com
Hours Mar. 15–Second Sunday in Nov., 9 a.m. to 6 p.m.
Fee Yes

As part of the Blue Spring Heritage Center, which celebrates Native American heritage in the Ozarks, Eureka Springs Gardens took root in 1993. Featured is the Medicine Wheel Garden, which is planted as a circle divided into four sections. Other gardens include the Three Sisters and Woodland.

Balboa Park Garden

Address 1549 El Prado, San Diego, 92101
Phone (619) 239-0512
Website www.balboapark.org/in-the-park/gardens
Hours Daily
Fee No

The Botanical Building, flanked by the Victorian-style lily pond, is among the most photographed scenes of the garden. Noteworthy gardens include the California Native Plants Garden, which showcases drought-tolerant natives suitable for home use. The WorldBeat Center's Children's Garden is a blend of herb, fruit, and vegetable gardens that honor the memory of George Washington Carver. Some gardens and other venues within the park, such as the Japanese Garden, have admission fees and set hours.

Filoli Garden

Address 86 Canada Rd., Woodside, 94062

Phone (650) 364-8300, ext. 507

Website www.filoli.org

Hours Tuesday–Saturday, 10 a.m. to 3:30 p.m.;
Sunday, 11 a.m. to 3:30 p.m.

Fee Yes

The house is an exhibit of seventeenth- and eighteenth-century English decorative arts and antiques. The Butler's Pantry and Kitchen with a walk-in safe are of special interest too. Food is also part of the gardens with a Gentlemen's Orchard, Olive Orchard, and citrus collection. Historically, the Service Courtyard was a kitchen and herb garden, but now it houses a retail nursery. The West Terraces link the house to the garden with long, paved walkways. The Main Axis is designed to take advantage of Crystal Spring Lake.

Ganna Walska Lotusland Garden

Address 695 Ashley Rd., Santa Barbara, 93108
Phone (805) 969-9990
Website www.lotusland.org
Hours Only by reservation
Fee Yes

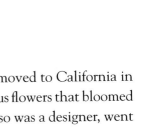

Walska was a Polish opera singer and actress who moved to California in 1941. Ultimately, she named the estate after the lotus flowers that bloomed in the ponds. Almost immediately, Walska, who also was a designer, went about creating a botanical garden working with various architects and landscape architects. In the 1960s, a Japanese Garden was created. In all 18 gardens and types of collections adorn the grounds, including a topiary garden, theatre garden, and blue garden.

Hearst Castle Gardens

Address 750 Hearst Castle Rd., San Simeon, 93452
Phone (800) 444-4445 or TDD (800) 274-7275, or
outside U.S. (518) 218-5078
Website www.hearstcastle.com
Hours Daily
Fee Yes; reservations strongly recommended

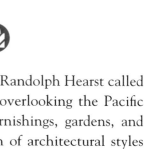

Architect Julia Morgan designed what William Randolph Hearst called "the ranch," an elaborate complex on a bluff overlooking the Pacific Ocean. The castle, its decorative arts and furnishings, gardens, and grounds are an extravagant, eclectic collection of architectural styles and periods. Colorful flowers such as bougainvillea, hyacinths, gladiolus, lilies, dahlias, geraniums, sweet peas, hollyhocks, and tulips are some of the many varieties grown. Thousands of annuals, bulbs, and perennials are planted each year to provide the color displays Hearst enjoyed in his gardens.

Huntington Botanical Gardens

Address 1151 Oxford Rd., San Marino, 91108

Phone (626) 405-2100

Website www.huntington.org

Hours Summer, Wednesday–Monday, 10:30 a.m. to 4:30 p.m.;
After Labor Day, Monday, Wednesday–Friday, noon to
4:30 p.m., Saturday–Sunday, 10:30 a.m. to 4:30 p.m.

Fee Yes; free the first Thursday of the month with advance ticket

Originally 600 acres, the Huntington Gardens now cover 207 acres, of which about 120 are landscaped. The gardens have more than 14,000 varieties of plants displayed in 12 major areas. Among the themed areas are Australian, Camellia, Children's, Chinese, Desert, Herb, Japanese, Jungle, Lily Pond, Palm, Rose, and Shakespeare gardens. Several gardens change each year with new plantings. In the 16,000-square-foot Rose Hills Foundation Conservatory is an *Amorphophallus titanum* plant, commonly referred to as the corpse flower because of the stench of the blooms.

Los Angeles County Arboretum & Botanical Garden

Address 301 N. Baldwin Ave., Arcadia, 91007
Phone (626) 821-3222
Website www.arboretum.org
Hours 9 a.m. to 5 p.m. daily
Fee Yes

This 127-acre botanical garden and historic site occupies the heart of the Rancho Santa Anna. It is home to plant collections from around the world, including many rare and endangered species. On the grounds are several historical landmarks, such as the Queen Anne Cottage, built in 1885, which remains an ornate example of Victorian lakeside landscape. The Garden for All Seasons is an interactive display of wildflowers, herbs, and vegetables that is used as an all-season classroom.

Rancho Santa Ana Botanic Garden

Address 1500 N. College Ave., Claremont, 91711
Phone (909) 625-8767
Website www.rsabg.org
Hours 8 a.m. to 5 p.m. daily
Fee Yes

One of this garden's conservation efforts is Hooker's manzanita, a California native, which is extinct in the wild. Cuttings of the plant have been sent to the Royal Botanic Gardens at Kew, a repository of all plants, and seeds, to the Millennium Seed Bank. About half of the garden's 86 acres are dedicated to California natives, planted in gardens designed to emulate native habitats. Aside from its academic endeavors, the garden, started in 1927, demonstrates how to use native plants in the home landscape.

CALIFORNIA

San Diego Botanic Garden

Address 230 Quail Gardens Dr., Encinitas, 92024
Phone (760) 436-3036
Website www.sdbgarden.org
Hours 9 a.m. to 5 p.m. daily, until 8 p.m. on Thursdays in summer
Fee Yes

One of the spectacular plantings at this garden is the timber bamboo, which visitors can almost hear growing as they stand among the culms. Formerly called the Quail Botanical Gardens, the Hamilton Children's Garden is known to have a quail or two scurrying about. Other exhibits include low-water plants and fire-safe landscaping techniques. The garden, which represents 15 different regions, also conserves native plants, such as southern maritime chaparral and coastal sage, which are threatened because of habitat development.

San Francisco Botanical Garden at Strybing Arboretum

Address 9th Ave. at Lincoln Way, San Francisco, 94122

Phone (415) 661-1316

Website www.sfbotanicalgarden.org

Hours Apr.–Oct., 9 a.m. to 6 p.m.; Nov.–Mar., daily, 10 a.m. to 5 p.m.

Fee Yes; free the second Tuesday of the month and certain holidays

The region's mild Mediterranean climate provides the gardens with perfect conditions to grow and conserve plants from all over the world, including plants that are no longer found in their native habitats. There are more than 55 acres of sanctuary, landscaped gardens, and open spaces with more than 8,000 types of plants. Display gardens and special collections include a perennial garden, Meso American and Southeast Asian cloud forests, a moon viewing garden, succulent garden, native plant gardens of many countries, and a garden of fragrance.

CALIFORNIA

University of California Berkeley Botanical Garden

Address 200 Centennial Dr., Berkeley, 94720
   Phone (510) 643-2755
Website www.botanicalgarden.berkeley.edu
   Hours 9 a.m. to 5 p.m., closed the first Tuesday of the month
      Fee Yes; free the first Thursday of the month

Established in 1890, the garden holds more than 13,000 kinds of plants from around the world, organized regionally on 34 acres that overlook the campus. An emphasis of the garden is on plants that thrive in the California climate, such as those from the Mediterranean, Australia, Chile, and South Africa. Greenhouses contain arid, carnivorous, and orchid plants. Gardens of particular interest include Chinese Medicinal Herb, Crops of the World, and Garden of Old Roses.

Casa del Herrero

Address 1387 E. Valley Rd., Santa Barbara, 92101
Phone (805) 565-5653
Website www.casadelherrero.com
Hours Mid-Feb.–mid-Nov., by advance registration only
Fee Yes

The House of the Blacksmith's gardens, many of which have a Moorish influence, are arid or lush, depending on the plantings, and beautifully decorated with tiles and other material. This property is on the National Register of Historic Places and is considered a National Historic Landmark.

Conejo Valley Botanic Garden

Address 350 W. Gainsborough Rd., Thousand Oaks, 91360
Phone (805) 494-7630
Website www.conejogarden.org
Hours 7 a.m. to 5 p.m. daily, except special hours for holidays
Fee No

Unique, rugged terrain makes up this 33-acre garden, most of which is dedicated to natural habitat for native plants and animals. There are designated garden areas, including the Butterfly Garden, Tranquility Garden, and Rare Fruit Garden. The Kids' Adventure Garden has slightly different hours; call ahead.

Conservatory of Flowers

Address 100 John F. Kennedy Dr., San Francisco, 94118
Phone (415) 831-2090
Website www.conservatoryofflowers.org
Hours Tuesday–Sunday, 10 a.m. to 4:30 p.m.
Fee Yes, free the first Tuesday of the month

The conservatory has permanent collections of aquatic, highland tropics, lowland tropics, and potted plants. One section is devoted to special exhibits. In the Aquatic Plants house, massive Amazon water lilies cover the pond, which is surrounded by carnivorous plants, bromeliads, and tropical orchids.

Descanso Gardens

Address 1418 Descanso Dr., La Cañada Flintridge, 91011
Phone (818) 949-4200
Website www.descansogardens.org
Hours 9 a.m. to 5 p.m.
Fee Yes

The Japanese Garden's koi-filled stream flows to the Full Moon Tea House to create a traditional strolling meditation garden. To showcase native Southern California plants, an 8-acre garden was created in 1959. There are also camellia, iris, lilac, and rose gardens.

Earl Burns Miller Japanese Garden

Address 1250 Bellflower Blvd., California State University at Long Beach, Long Beach, 90840
Phone (562) 985-8885
Website www.csulb.edu/~jgarden
Hours Tuesday–Friday, 8 a.m. to 3:30 p.m., Sunday, noon to 4 p.m.
Fee No

The donors of this garden wanted a garden where people could go when they were tired, anxious, or seeking beauty. Their hope was that visitors would leave refreshed and ready for the day. The $1^{1}/_{3}$-acre hill and pond garden achieves that for thousands of visitors each year.

Elizabeth Gamble Garden

Address 1431 Waverley St., Palo Alto, 94301
Phone (650) 329-1356
Website www.gamblegarden.org
Hours Daily, daylight
Fee No

The $2^{1}/_{2}$-acre Edwardian estate includes a historic home, gardens, carriage house, and tea house. Wisterias are grown as small trees behind the house and as well as allée of flowering cherry trees. Magnolias, rhododendrons, and camellias add fantastic color to the woodland garden.

CALIFORNIA

Forrest Deanery Native Plant Botanic Garden

Address One State Park Rd., Benicia, 94510
Phone (707) 747-6204
Website www.cnpsjepsonchapter.homestead.com/botgard.html
Hours 8 a.m. to sunset, daily
Fee Yes

The garden, which specializes in native plants, overlooks the Sacramento and San Joaquin rivers. The gardens are cared for by the Willis L. Jepson Chapter of the California Native Plant Society. The butterfly garden includes the California dutchman's pipe, a favorite food of the pipe-vine swallowtail.

Fullerton Arboretum

Address 1900 Associated Rd., Fullerton, 92831
Phone (657) 278-3407
Website www.fullertonarboretum.org
Hours 8 a.m. to 4:30 p.m. daily, extended hours in summer
Fee Donation requested

The 26-acre arboretum opened in 1979 and contains 4,000 unique and unusual plant species from around the world. The grounds are also home to the Orange County Agricultural and Nikkei Heritage Museum and an El Camino Real Bell.

Gardens at Heather Farm

Address 1540 Marchbanks Dr., Walnut Creek, 94598
Phone (925) 947-1678
Website www.gardenshf.org
Hours Daily, daylight hours
Fee No fee for self-guided tours

More than 1,000 roses bloom without the use of any pesticides, a sustainable practice followed throughout the 6-acre educational center. The property is a Certified Wildlife Habitat and Certified Green Business. The Black Pine Garden is a bonsai display.

Getty Center

Address 1200 Getty Center Dr., Los Angeles, 90049
Phone (310) 440-7300
Website www.getty.edu
Hours Tuesday–Friday and Sunday, 10 a.m. to 5:30 p.m.; Saturday until 9 p.m.
Fee No

The 134,000-square-foot Central Garden is the heart of the Getty Center. It takes visitors through plantings of more than 500 native and exotic species. Many of the plants are aromatic or have unusual textures, and water sounds add to the visitor's experience. There's also a museum and renowned art gallery at the Getty Villa in Malibu.

Hakone Gardens

Address 21000 Big Basin Way, Saratoga, 95070
Phone (408) 741-4994
Website www.hakone.com
Hours Weekdays 10 a.m. to 5 p.m.; weekends, 11 a.m. to 5 p.m.
Fee No

Established in 1915, Hakone is the site of the oldest Japanese and Asian estate gardens in the Western Hemisphere and is designated a National Trust for Historic Preservation. Located in the Saratoga Hills, Hakone occupies more than 18 acres consisting of chaparral, woodland, and manicured Japanese gardens.

Hortense Miller Garden

Address 22511 Allview Terrace, Laguna Beach, 92651
Phone (949) 497-0716
Website www.hortensemillergarden.org
Hours Tuesday–Saturday, 9:45 a.m. to noon, reservations only through Laguna Beach Recreations Department
Fee No

The Hortense Miller Garden, established in 1959, covers 2^1/$_2$ acres of the upper slopes of Boat Canyon in Laguna Beach. The garden, which surrounds a mid-century modern home, demonstrates the range of plants that can be grown in Southern California coastal zones.

Humboldt Botanical Garden

Address 2436 Sixth St., Eureka, 95501
Phone (707) 442-5139
Website ww.hbgf.org
Hours Daily
Fee No

Although much of the garden is still under construction, several areas have been planted. The garden is especially interested in maintaining complete native conifer, iris, and lily collections. The propagating and growing of the endangered *Lilium occidentale* (Western lily) in the Native Garden is one effort.

Japanese Friendship Garden

Address 2215 Pan American Rd. E., San Diego, 92101
Phone (619) 232-2721
Website www.niwa.org
Hours Memorial Day–Labor Day, Monday–Friday, 10 a.m. to 5 p.m., Saturday–Sunday, 10 a.m. to 4 p.m.; fall, winter and spring, Tuesday–Sunday, 10 a.m. to 4 p.m.
Fee Yes

The design of the Japanese Friendship Garden is guided by the original principles of a Japanese garden, while incorporating the regional landscape and climate. The garden is in Balboa Park, which has many amenities and other cultural venues, including a zoo and museum.

The Japanese Garden

Address 6100 Woodley Ave., Van Nuys, 91406
Phone (818) 765-8166
Website www.thejapanesegarden.com
Hours Monday–Thursday, 11 a.m. to 4 p.m.; Sunday, 10 a.m. to 4 p.m.
Fee Yes

Dubbed "the garden of water and fragrance," its narrow entry is designed so that only two people can enter at a time. The garden is adorned with Japanese lanterns, stones, and benches where visitors sit to contemplate.

Luther Burbank Home and Gardens

Address 204 Santa Rosa Ave., Santa Rosa, 95402
Phone (707) 524-5445
Website www.lutherburbank.org
Hours Apr.–Oct., 8 a.m. to dusk
Fee Yes

This is the home, garden, and greenhouse of Luther Burbank, one of the best-known plant breeders in the world. The year 2011 was the 110th anniversary of his introduction of the Shasta daisy, named after Mt. Shasta. There are four specialty gardens, including a spineless cacti garden containing 60 species bred by Burbank. The other specialty gardens include medicinal, edible landscape, and wildlife gardens.

Markham Nature Park and Arboretum

Address 1202 La Vista Ave., Concord, 94521
Phone (925) 681-2968
Website www.markhamarboretum.org
Hours Daily, daylight
Fee No

Begun in 1981, the 16-acre arboretum is still being developed and much of it remains in a natural, but slightly tamed state. The International Garden on the grounds exhibits a large variety of trees, shrubs, and vines arranged by country of origin. The Tree Walk showcases 45 of the 90 different tree species.

Mendocino Coast Botanical Gardens

Address 18220 N. Hwy. One, Fort Bragg, 95437
Phone (707) 964-4352
Website www.gardenbythesea.org
Hours Mar.–Oct., 9 a.m. to 5 p.m.; Nov.–Feb., 9 a.m. to 4 p.m.
Fee Yes

The gardens are known for their rhododendrons native to the cloud forests of Southeast Asia and the Himalayas, which produce some of the most fragrant blossoms. There is also a collection of heaths and heathers, and perennials borders planted for the seasons. The Quail Trail is a "treasure hunt" oriented toward children.

Mildred E. Mathias Garden at UCLA

Address 100 Stein Plaza, Los Angeles, 90095
Phone (310) 825-1260
Website www.botgard.ucla.edu
Hours Monday–Friday, 8 a.m. to 5 p.m.; Saturday–Sunday 8 a.m. to 4 p.m.
Fee No, but parking permit needed

The 7-acre garden contains North America's tallest dawn redwood, grown from seed in 1941. The garden honors Mathias, a well-known horticulturist, who was concerned about the destruction of rain forests. Special collections include lilies, rhododendrons, bromeliads, ferns, and plants native to Hawaii. There are about 5,000 species of 225 families on display.

Moorten Botanical Gardens

Address 1701 S. Palm Canyon Dr., Palm Springs, 92264
Phone (760) 327-6555
Website www.moortengarden.com
Hours 10 a.m. to 4 p.m. daily, except Wednesday
Fee No

The garden, which started in 1938, is devoted to desert plants. More than 3,000 varieties of desert cacti and plants, from giants to miniatures, are arranged in appropriate habitats along a natural trail. The garden is also rich with fossils, colorful rocks, and pioneer relics. The "Cactarium" greenhouse also includes succulents.

CALIFORNIA

Quarryhill Botanical Garden

Address 12841 Sonoma Hwy. (Rt. 12), Glen Ellen, 95442
Phone (707) 996-6027
Website www.quarryhillbg.org
Hours 9 a.m. to 4 p.m. daily
Fee Yes

Founded in 1987, this 20-acre garden is home to one of the largest collections of scientifically documented, wild-sourced Asian plants in North America and Europe. Several collections are rare or endangered species.

Regional Parks Botanic Garden

Address Wildcat Canyon Rd. and Grizzly Peak Blvd., Tilden Regional Park, Berkeley, 94708
Phone (510) 544-3169
Website www.nativeplants.org
Hours June 1–Sept. 30, 8:30 a.m. to 5:30 p.m.; Oct. 1–May 31, 8:30 a.m. to 5 p.m.
Fee No

The 10-acre garden is a living museum of California native plants. It provides a sanctuary for many of the state's rare and endangered specimens. Included are species from the High Sierra, serpentine barrens of the Coast Ranges, northern rain forests, and southern deserts. There are flowers blooming every month.

Ruth Bancroft Garden

Address 1552 Bancroft Rd., Walnut Creek, 94598
Phone (925) 944-9352 or (925) 210-9663
Website www.ruthbancroftgarden.org
Hours 10 a.m. to 4 p.m. daily
Fee Yes

This is a water-conserving garden featuring plants appropriate for California's Mediterranean climate. The garden also houses important collections of aloes, agaves, yuccas, and echeverias. *Aeonium* 'Glenn Davidson', the first succulent in Ruth Bancroft's collection, is still growing there.

Santa Barbara Botanic Garden

Address 1212 Mission Canyon Rd., Santa Barbara, 93105
Phone (805) 682-4726
Website www.sbbg.org
Hours Mar.–Oct., 9 a.m. to 6 p.m. daily
Fee Yes

More than 1,000 native species are planted in this premier garden, which is accessible by 5¹/₂ miles of public trails. The Smith Herbarium houses 143,000 specimens used for research. The 78-acre site features themed gardens overlooking the Channel Islands.

South Coast Botanic Garden

Address 26300 Crenshaw Blvd., Palos Verdes Peninsula, 90274
Phone (310) 544-1948
Website www.southcoastbotanicgarden.org
Hours 9 a.m. to 5 p.m. daily
Fee Yes

More than 200,000 plants cover the grounds of the gardens, including the 3 Bears House Children's Garden. Other displays of dahlias, fuchsias, roses, Mediterranean plants, cacti, water-wise gardening, and a garden for the senses entice you to linger. There's also a Japanese garden and koi pond.

Sunset Garden

Address 80 Willow Rd., Menlo Park, 94025
Phone (650) 321-3600
Website www.sunset.com/garden/landscaping-design/sunset-garden-tour-00400000015024
Hours 9 a.m. to 4 p.m. workdays
Fee No

The self-guided tour takes visitors through the gardens surrounding Sunset headquarters. The gardens demonstrate landscapes and plants for the six West Coast climates, from the Pacific Northwest to Southern California, and a 3,000-square-foot test garden.

CALIFORNIA

Turtle Bay Exploration Park's McConnell Arboretum and Botanical Gardens

Address 840 Sundial Bridge Dr., Redding, 96003
Phone (800) 887-8532
Website www.turtlebay.org
Hours 7 a.m. to 7 p.m. daily in summer, various in winter
Fee Yes

The 20-acre garden is the newest addition to the park. Displays cover the Mediterranean climate, a children's garden, a medicinal garden, and two beautiful and unique water features. The arboretum extends over 200 acres with direct links to the award-winning Sacramento River Trail.

University of California, Davis Arboretum

Address Valley Oak Cottage, LaRue Rd., Davis, 95616
Phone (530) 752-4880
Website www.arboretum.ucdavis.edu
Hours 24 hours a day
Fee No for admission; fee for parking weekdays

The 100-acre arboretum contains 22,000 trees and plants adapted to a Mediterranean climate of hot, dry summers and cool, wet winters. Exhibits in the demonstration gardens highlight sustainable horticulture, native plants, the coast redwood, and an oak grove.

University of California, Riverside Botanic Gardens

Address Botanic Gardens Dr., Riverside, 92507
Phone (951) 784-6962
Website www.gardens.ucr.edu
Hours 8 a.m. to 5 p.m.
Fee Yes

Vistas of the San Bernardino and San Gabriel mountains serve as the backdrop for the 40-acre garden of rugged, hilly terrain in the foothills of the Box Springs Mountains. Situated on the eastern border of the campus, the gardens include plants from Baja, the Sierra foothills, and Southwest desert.

Virginia Robinson Gardens

Address 1008 Elden Way, Beverly Hills, 90210
Phone (310) 550-2065
Website www.robinsongardens.org
Hours Tuesday–Friday by appointment only
Fee Yes

This property dates to 1911 and the birth of luxury estates in Beverly Hills. Although the house is on the Garden Benefit Tour, people really come here to enjoy the six sloping acres of gardens, from the Australian King Palm Forest to the Rose Garden and Italian Terrace Garden.

Water Conservation Garden

Address 12122 Cuyamaca College Dr. West, El Cajon, 92019
Phone (619) 660-0614
Website www.thegarden.org
Hours 9 a.m. to 4 p.m., daily, until 7 p.m. Wednesdays in summer
Fee No

Here are five acres of displays that exemplify water conservation in themed gardens. Exhibits feature a meadow, cacti and succulents, turf, a white garden, groundcover, vegetables, compost, containers, native plants, sensory plants, children's discovery trail, firewise and water-wise landscaping, and more.

Wrigley Memorial Botanic Garden on Catalina Island

Address Avalon Canyon Rd., Avalon, 90704
Phone (310) 510-2595
Website www.catalina.com/memorial.html
Hours 8 a.m. to 5 p.m. daily
Fee Yes

The garden was started in 1935 by Ada Wrigley, wife of the founder of the chewing gum company. At the center of the 38-acre garden is a gorgeous view of Avalon Bay. Since the late 1960s, the garden has focused on California island native plants. Many are extremely rare species.

Betty Ford Alpine Garden

Address 530 S. Frontage Rd., Vail, 81657
Phone (970) 476-0103
Website www.bettyfordalpinegardens.org
Hours dawn to dusk
Fee No, donations requested

At 8,200 feet above sea level, the Betty Ford Alpine Garden claims to be the world's highest botanic garden. It features 3,000 species of alpine, mountain, and sub-mountain plants from the Rocky Mountains and elsewhere in garden and natural settings. The garden in the Gerald R. Ford Park is divided into four sections: Mountain Perennial Garden, Mountain Meditation Garden, Alpine Rock Garden, and Children's Garden. The garden also has a horticulture therapy program in the Schoolhouse Garden.

Denver Botanic Gardens

Address 1007 York St., Denver, 80206
Phone (720) 865-3500
Website www.botanicgardens.org
Hours May–Sept., 9 a.m. to 9 p.m.; Oct.–Apr., 9 a.m. to 5 p.m.
Fee Yes

The gardens feature plants and landscape designs from around the world, but specialize in native plants from Colorado. The garden features nearly three dozen themed gardens, including water, children's, alpine, endangered species, herbs, birds and bees walk, perennials, ornamental grasses, shade, romantic and an All-America Selections garden. There's even a section for community gardeners. The Boettcher Memorial Tropical Conservatory has a two-story model of a banyan tree, which gives visitors an aerial view of the tropical forest below. The gardens also have regular art exhibits and concerts.

Colorado Springs Utilities Xeriscape Demonstration Garden

Address 2855 Mesa Rd., Colorado Springs, 80904
Phone (719) 668-4555
Website www.csu.org/wa/xeri/xeriscape.jsp
Hours Business hours
Fee No

This garden demonstrates the seven principles of Xeriscape, which fosters landscape design that relies on plants with low-water needs. Plants, most of which come from the Colorado Springs area, are grouped by their water requirements.

Western Colorado Botanical Gardens

Address 641 Struthers Ave., Grand Junction, 81501
Phone (970) 245-9030
Website www.wcbotanic.org
Hours Tuesday–Sunday, 10 a.m. to 5:30 p.m.
Fee Yes

Founded by the Western Colorado Botanical Garden in 1994, this 15-acre garden was built by volunteers to profile the Colorado River Basin and Plateau. It has a butterfly house and herb, cactus, rose, and orchid displays. There's also a Children's Secret Garden.

Garden of Ideas

Address 647 N. Salem Rd., Ridgefield, 06877
Phone (203) 431-9914
Website www.gardenofideas.com
Hours 8 a.m. to 7 p.m. daily
Fee No

Twelve acres of sculpture-adorned gardens include a botanical plant collection, vegetable production, and woody and herbaceous plants with a few tropicals and annuals mixed in. Foodies and nature and bird enthusiasts will appreciate the marshland, which supports an annual crop of wild rice. The gardens are owned by a family who also operates a certified organic vegetable farm. A restoration is underway of a woodland, which is designed to guide homeowners who have shady landscapes or deer pressure.

Bartlett Arboretum & Gardens

Address 151 Brookdale Rd., Stamford, 06903
Phone (203) 322-6971
Website www.bartlettarboretum.org
Hours 9 a.m. to 7 p.m.
Fee Yes; no fee Wednesdays

The former property of Francis A. Bartlett, founder of Bartlett Tree Experts, these 91 acres encompass award-winning champion trees, charming gardens, wildflower meadows, red maple wetlands and boardwalks, woodland walking trails, varied wildlife, and native habitats.

Glebe House & Gertrude Jekyll Garden

Address 49 Hollow Rd., Woodbury, 06798
Phone (203) 263-2855
Website www.theglebehouse.org
Hours May–Oct., Wednesday–Sunday, 1 p.m. to 4 p.m.;
Nov., 1 p.m. to 4 p.m., weekends
Fee Yes

The Episcopal Church in the United States was founded at Glebe House in the 1770s. In the 1920s, renowned English landscape designer Gertrude Jekyll created a garden around what is now a museum, developing a 600-foot English garden border, a rose allée, and foundation plantings. This is the only extant American garden planned by Jekyll.

DELAWARE

Delaware Center for Horticulture

Address 1810 N. Dupont St., Wilmington, 19806
Phone (302) 658-6262
Website www.thedch.org
Hours Dawn to dusk
Fee No

If you are looking for plants and designs for urban and suburban landscapes, this is the place. Created with an eye toward sustainable practices, the gardens have sculpture and other items made of recycled or found objects. On the grounds is the Community Gallery at DCH, which exhibits art with environmental or horticultural themes. The center also coordinates a citywide garden contest, some of which may be seen from street tours. A big draw for plant enthusiasts is the Rare Plant Auction held the last Saturday in April. An extensive horticulture library is open to the public.

Mt. Cuba Center

Address 3120 Barley Mill Rd., Hockessin, 19707

Phone (302) 239-4244

Website www.mtcubacenter.org

Hours By reservation

Fee Yes

Known far and wide for its woodland plants and wildflowers, Mt. Cuba is the former estate of the duPont-Copeland family. A two-hour tour includes the estate's formal gardens, pastures, fields, and woodland landscapes. Tours are held rain or shine, except in extreme weather, in spring, summer, and fall.

Nemours Mansion & Gardens

Address 850 Alapocas Dr., Wilmington, 19803

Phone (800) 651-6912

Website www.nemoursmansion.org

Hours May 1–Dec. 31, tours on Tuesday–Saturday, 9 a.m., noon and 3 p.m., tours on Sunday, noon and 3 p.m.

Fee Yes

Reservations are recommended for the two-hour tour of the former estate of Alfred I. duPont. The formal and naturalistic landscapes are rich with French-inspired, ornate sculptures and fountains. The property underwent a $39 million restoration a few years ago. A one-acre pool contains 157 jets shooting water 12 feet into the air.

University of Delaware Botanic Gardens

Address 531 S. College Ave., Newark, 19716
Phone (302) 831-0153
Website www.ag.udel.edu/udbg
Hours Sunrise to sunset, daily
Fee No

Part of the College of Agriculture & Natural Resources, the botanic garden is known for its color trials and as an All-America Selections test garden in the Herbaceous Garden. There are also a native plant garden, greenhouses, and wetlands. It is a four-season garden.

Winterthur Museum, Garden & Library

Address 5105 Kennett Pike (Rt. 52), Wilmington, 19807
Phone (800) 448-3883; TTY (302) 888-4907
Website www.winterthur.org
Hours Tuesday–Sunday, 10 a.m. to 5 p.m.
Fee Yes

Reservations are required to tour Winterthur, the childhood home and gardens of Henry Francis duPont. Winterthur is as well known for its collection of American decorative arts as its landscapes, which span 1,000 acres. The 60-acre gardens, designed by duPont, exemplify American Country Estate living.

Hillwood Estate, Museum & Gardens

Address 4155 Linnean Ave. NW, Washington, D.C., 20008
Phone (202) 686-5807
Website www.hillwoodmuseum.org
Hours Feb.–Dec., Tuesday–Saturday, 10 a.m. to 5 p.m., and select Sundays
Fee Yes

Marjorie Merriweather Post, the famous heiress, businesswoman, diplomat, and art collector, lived in this Georgian home, which is on the fringe of Rock Creek Park. The gardens, adorned with sculpture and other art, include a French parterre, four-season overlook, Japanese, and cutting gardens. Her ashes are buried in the rose garden, designed by Perry Wheeler, who also designed the White House Rose Garden. From the Lunar Lawn you can see the Washington Monument.

United States Botanic Garden

Address 100 Maryland Ave. SW, Washington, D.C., 20001
Phone (202) 225-8333
Website www.usbg.gov
Hours Conservatory, 10 a.m. to 5 p.m. daily; National Garden,
May 28–Sept. 5, 10 a.m. to 7 p.m. daily; Bartholdi Park,
dawn to dusk daily
Fee No

The U.S. Botanic Garden maintains 26,000 plants, including historic, medicinal, orchids, succulents, cycads, and ferns. The National Garden is a living laboratory that features contemplative settings, a butterfly garden, lawn terrace, herbs, perennials, regional plantings, and the First Ladies' Water Garden. The 28,944-square-foot conservatory contains a collection that spans 150 years in botany, economic and cultural history. There's also a Children's Garden and an exhibit that shows how plants have adapted to their environment. Parking is extremely limited, but it is easily accessible by public transportation.

Dumbarton Oaks

Address 1703 32nd St. NW, Washington, D.C., 20007
Phone (202) 339-6401
Website www.doaks.org
Hours Mar. 15–Oct. 3, Tuesday–Sunday, 12 p.m. to 6 p.m.
Fee Yes

From the 1920s to the 1950s, owner Mildred Bliss worked with the famous American landscaper Beatrix Farrand to develop garden rooms, terraces, a cutting garden, food garden, recreational, and natural areas. The home was the setting for the groundwork in the formation of the United Nations.

U.S. National Arboretum

Address 3501 New York Ave., NE, Washington, D.C., 20002
Phone (202) 245-2726
Website www.usna.usda.gov
Hours 8 a.m. to 5 p.m. daily
Fee No

The arboretum, which has introduced more than 650 plants, contains the National Grove of State Trees and collections of perennials, boxwoods, dogwoods, azaleas, and the National Bonsai and Penjing Museum. There is ample free parking. A 35-minute tram tour is available for a fee with reservations.

Edison & Ford Winter Estates

Address 2350 McGregor Blvd., Fort Myers, 33901
Phone (239) 334-7419
Website www.edisonfordwinterestates.org
Hours 9 a.m. to 5:30 p.m. daily
Fee Yes

The neighboring estates have more than 1,700 plants, representing 400 species from six continents, including champion trees, a large banyan tree that covers an acre, an allée of royal palms, a citrus grove, a cycad collection, and heritage plants planted by Edison and Ford. There's also a vegetable garden that reflects crops grown by the families for their tables. The grounds also demonstrate Edison's interest in the garden as a botanical laboratory. The houses are the rambling type of vacation homes, with guesthouses, caretakers' cottages, and pools.

Fairchild Tropical Botanic Garden

Address 10901 Old Cutler Rd., Coral Gables, 33156
Phone (305) 667-1651
Website www.fairchildgarden.org
Hours 9:30 a.m. to 4:30 p.m. daily
Fee Yes

Since 1938, the Fairchild Tropical Botanic Garden has been an orchestrated blend of art and science with an outstanding collection of well-documented tropical plants, especially palms, cycads, flowering trees and shrubs, vines, and fruit trees. Besides their world significance, the plants and their beauty have earned the 83-acre Fairchild top marks as a major cultural attraction, as well as offering a basis for education, research, and conservation of tropical plants and birds. A 16,428-square-foot conservatory and its 1,900 plants serve as a window on the humid tropics.

Harry P. Leu Gardens

Address 1920 N. Forest Ave., Orlando, 32803
Phone (407) 246-2620
Website www.leugardens.org
Hours 9 a.m. to 5 p.m.
Fee Yes, but free the first Monday of the month

Nearly two dozen gardens or collections make up the 40-acre Leu Gardens, the former home of a local businessman and philanthropist. Plants are changed every four months in the Annual Garden, which is filled with annuals, perennials, and colorful shrubs and other plants. Leu also has collections of daylilies, bananas, bamboos, bromeliads, crape myrtles, gingers, false bird of paradise, and conifers. The Home Demonstration Garden offers ideas for all kinds of gardens, from fragrance to bogs.

Marie Selby Botanical Gardens

Address 811 S. Palm Ave., Sarasota, 34236
Phone (941) 366-5731
Website www.selby.org
Hours 10 a.m. to 5 p.m. daily
Fee Yes

The Gardens maintain a collection of more than 20,000 greenhouse plants, plus thousands more outdoors. Eight greenhouses include the stunning Tropical Conservatory, where unusual plants and flowers can be seen year-round. Its specialty as a botanic garden is epiphytes. It takes about two hours to tour the gardens, which have various themes: wildflower, cycad, fragrance, hibiscus, bamboo, bromeliad, butterfly, palm grove, tidal lagoon, and bonsai. The Mediterranean Revival-style Selby home serves as a restaurant.

Albin Polasek Museum & Sculpture Gardens

Address 633 Osceola Ave., Winter Park, 32789
  Phone (407) 647-6294
Website www.polasek.org
  Hours Tuesday–Sunday, 10 a.m. to 4 p.m.; Sunday, 1 p.m. to 4 p.m.
    Fee Yes

More than 200 pieces of Polasek's sculpture adorn the gardens, which date to 1949. Trees, shrubs, and other plants are labeled and there are special sections, including a butterfly garden, two water gardens, a cycad collection, and many container gardens.

American Orchid Society Visitors Center & Botanical Garden

Address 16700 AOS Lane, Delray Beach, 33446
  Phone (561) 404-2000
Website www.aos.org
    Hours 8 a.m. to 5 p.m.
      Fee Yes, for the Gardens; orchid display free

The 3-acre garden includes a 4,000 square-foot greenhouse where orchid displays change monthly. Inside and out, orchids are displayed as they would be found in nature. This is an easy way to appreciate all of the forms, habits, colors, and fragrances that orchids have to offer.

Bok Tower Gardens

Address 1151 Tower Blvd., Lake Wales, 33884
Phone (863) 676-1408
Website www.boktowergardens.org
Hours 8 a.m. to 5 p.m. daily
Fee Yes

Designed by Frederick Law Olmsted, the 250-acre botanical garden includes the 205-foot tall Singer Tower, a neo-Gothic, Art Deco style carillon that offers daily concerts. Olmsted planted hundreds of oaks, palms, magnolias, and azaleas on one of the highest points in central Florida. There are many family friendly areas.

Bonnet House Museum & Gardens

Address 900 N. Birch Rd., Fort Lauderdale, 33304
Phone (954) 563-5393
Website www.bonnethouse.org
Hours Tuesday–Saturday, 10 a.m. to 4 p.m., Sunday, 11 a.m. to 4 p.m.
Fee Yes

This 35-acre estate is a prime example of a native barrier island habitat with 5 ecosystems. The grounds contain an aviary with Amazon parrots and other birds, a large orchid collection, a mangrove wetlands, and other habitats for a variety of fish, monkeys, and other wildlife.

Jacksonville Zoo and Gardens

Address 370 Zoo Parkway, Jacksonville, 32218
 Phone (904) 757-4463
Website www.jacksonvillezoo.org
 Hours Daily, 9 a.m. to 5 p.m.; Mar. 5–Sept. 5, Monday–Friday, 9 a.m. to 5 pm.,
   Saturday–Sunday, 9 a.m. to 6 p.m.
  Fee Yes

The zoo has built its botanical garden amid the animal exhibits as a way
to continue its mission of conservation and preservation of species. The
three major garden zones are the River of Color, Themed Pocket Gardens
(several different gardens), and the Primary Garden.

Kanapaha Botanical Gardens

Address 4700 S.W. 58th Dr., Gainesville, 32608
 Phone (352) 372-4981
Website www.kanapaha.org
 Hours Monday–Wednesday, Friday, 9 a.m. to 5 p.m., Saturday–Sunday, 9 a.m. to dusk
  Fee Yes

Kanapaha Botanical Gardens has 24 major collections visually accessible
from a 1-mile paved walkway. Kanapaha's signature plants include a
premier stand of Chinese royal bamboo and during warm months, giant
Victoria water lilies and Asian snake arums. The best color comes from
June through September. The whimsical children's garden is sure to please.

Key West Tropical Forest & Botanical Garden

Address 5210 College Rd., Key West, 33040
  Phone (305) 296-1504
Website www.keywestbotanicalgarden.org
  Hours 10 a.m. to 4 p.m. daily
    Fee Yes

The only frost-free botanical garden in the continental United States, the Key West Botanical Garden's tropical rainfall allows plants to retain their leaves even during the dry winter season. The forest has two of the last remaining freshwater ponds in the Keys and is a major migratory stopping point for neo-tropical birds. It is home to many endangered plants.

Miami Beach Botanical Garden

Address 2000 Convention Center Dr., Miami Beach, 33139
  Phone (305) 673-7256
Website www.mbgarden.org
  Hours Tuesday–Sunday, 9 a.m. to 5 p.m.
    Fee No

This 4-acre botanical garden is a lovely green space in a heavily urban area. There's a Japanese Garden, collections of orchids and tropical plants, and a living wall (vertical landscape). The garden underwent a $1.2 million landscape renovation the summer of 2011.

McKee Botanical Garden

Address 350 U.S. Hwy. 1, Vero Beach, 32962
Phone (772) 794-0601
Website www.mckeegarden.org
Hours Tuesday–Saturday, 10 a.m. to 5 p.m., Sunday, noon to 5 p.m.
Fee Yes

The McKee Botanical Garden, known from the 1930s through the 1970s as the McKee Jungle Gardens, was resurrected after more than 20 years of vacancy, restored, and reopened in 2001. It's now an 18-acre paradise of tropical and sub-tropical plants, ponds, and water lilies.

Sunken Gardens

Address 1825 4th St. North, St. Petersburg, 33704
Phone (727)551-3102
Website www.stpete.org/sunken
Hours Monday–Saturday, 10 a.m. to 4:30 p.m., Sunday, noon to 4:30 p.m.
Fee Yes

In the middle of St. Pete sits the Sunken Gardens, a 100-year-old garden that is home to some of the oldest tropical plants in the region. The city's oldest living museum has meandering paths through 50,000 tropical plants and flowers, waterfalls, and demonstration gardens.

Atlanta Botanical Garden

Address 1345 Piedmont Ave. NE, Atlanta, 30309
Phone (404) 876-5859
Website www.atlantabotanicalgarden.org
Hours Apr.–Oct., Tuesday–Saturday, 9 a.m. to 7 p.m.; Nov.–Mar., 9 a.m. to 5 p.m.; May–Oct., Thursdays, 9 a.m. to 10 p.m.
Fee Yes

An expansion completed in 2010 doubled the size of the garden to 30 acres and included a new, green-roofed visitor center and a 600-foot-long canopy walk that winds through treetops 40 feet above the ground. Formal gardens welcome visitors at the entrance. Inside, visitors will find rose gardens, a Japanese garden, and woodland gardens. The 16,000-square-foot conservatory has a rainforest and the largest orchid exhibition on permanent display in the United States. The Children's Garden contains lessons about ecology, food, and plants.

State Botanical Garden of Georgia

Address 2450 S. Milledge Ave., Athens, 30605
Phone (706) 542-1244
Website www.uga.edu/botgarden
Hours Oct.–Mar., daily, 8 a.m. to 6 p.m.;
Apr.–Sept., daily, 8 a.m. to 8 p.m.
Fee No

This spectacular 300-acre garden serves as a living laboratory for the University of Georgia faculty, staff, and students. Gardens encompass native plants, shade, heritage, natural area, flowers, and an herb and physic garden. A native azalea collection and hybrid rhododendrons add to the beauty. The Heritage Garden celebrates Georgia's agrarian history, including development of the peach and pecan industries. The Tropical Conservatory, located in the Visitor Center, specializes in rainforest crops that can be harvested sustainably.

Callaway Gardens and Sibley Horticultural Center

Address 5887 Georgia Hwy 354, Pine Mountain, 31822
Phone (800) 225-5292
Website www.callawaygardens.com
Hours 9 a.m. to 6 p.m. daily; until 8 p.m. at the beach
Fee Yes

This one-of-a-kind garden and greenhouse encompasses 5 acres of native and exotic plants within its tropical conservatory, sub-Mediterranean conservatory, sculpture garden, fern grotto, main conservatory, and outdoor garden. Indoor displays are changed eight times a year, and outdoor displays at least five times. Don't miss the azalea trail in spring.

Massee Lane Gardens, American Camellia Society

Address 100 Massee Lane, Fort Valley, 31030
Phone (478) 967-2358 or (877) 422-6355
Website www.camellias-acs.com
Hours Tuesday–Saturday, 10 a.m. to 4:30 p.m., Sunday, 1 p.m. to 4:30 p.m.
Fee Yes

Massee Lane Gardens is a 100-acre botanical garden in middle Georgia, where camellias bloom from spring into fall. The gardens surround the historic home of the American Camellia Society. Besides a camellia garden, there are Japanese, rose, and environmental gardens.

Oak Hill & the Martha Berry Museum

Address 24 Veterans Memorial Hwy., Rome, 30161
Phone (706) 232-5374
Website www.berry.edu/oakhill
Hours 10 a.m. to 5 p.m.
Fee Yes

Martha Berry was the founder of Berry College, a four-year liberal arts college, in 1902. Opened as public gardens in 1972, it serves as an All-America Selections Demonstration Garden. There's also a sundial garden, formal garden, flowered pathway, and a goldfish garden.

Smith-Gilbert Gardens

Address 2382 Pine Mountain Rd., Kennesaw, 30152
Phone (770) 919-0248
Website www.smithgilbertgardens.com
Hours Monday–Saturday, 9 a.m. to 4 p.m., Sunday, 11 a.m. to 4 p.m.
Fee Yes

At the center of the gardens is the 150-year-old Hiram Butler Home and scattered through the 13 acres are more than 30 pieces of sculpture. The horticulture displays include a bonsai exhibit, camellia garden, teahouse and waterfall area, rose garden, and conifer display. More than 3,000 plants, many unique to American gardens, are on display.

Na`Āina Kai Botanical Gardens, Sculpture Park & Hardwood Plantation

Address 4101 Wallapa Rd., Kilauea, 96754

Phone (808) 828-0525

Website www.naainakai.org

Hours Tuesday–Saturday

Fee Yes

Trained docents guide all tours, which run 90 minutes to five hours. Tours can be on foot or in covered motorized vehicles. All tours include the Formal Garden, with its hedge maze, waterfall, and Japanese teahouse, palm garden, orchid house, and desert garden. Other tours cover a wild forest meadow, Kaluakai beach, and bird walk and marsh. "Under the Rainbow" Children's Garden tours are two hours.

Honolulu Botanical Gardens

Address Varies; 5 different gardens in different locations
Phone (808) 768-3003
Website www1.honolulu.gov/parks/hbg
Hours 9 a.m. to 4 p.m. daily
Fee No (except Foster Botanical Gardens)

Five gardens and locations make up the Honolulu Botanical Gardens, which specialize in native flora and tropical and sub-tropical plants. The Ho'omaluhia Botanical Garden houses the Hawaiian plants and ethnobotanical exhibits. Amenities vary by the garden.

University of Hawaii Lyon Arboretum and Botanical Garden

Address 3860 Manoa Rd., Honolulu, 96822
Phone (808) 988-0456
Website www.hawaii.edu/lyonarboretum
Hours Monday–Friday, 9 a.m. to 4 p.m., Saturday, 9 a.m. to 3 p.m.
Fee No

Founded in 1918, Lyon Arboretum is the only U.S. university arboretum located in a rainforest, where it rains 164 inches a year. Take rain gear and mosquito repellents for the hikes through 5,000 tropical plants. Nine different themed gardens are located throughout the 194-acre arboretum.

Idaho Botanical Garden

Address 2355 N. Old Penitentiary Rd., Boise, 83712
Phone (208) 343-8649
Website www.idahobotanicalgarden.org
Hours Mar. 14–Nov. 11, Monday, Wednesday–Friday, 9 a.m. to 5 p.m.,
Tuesday, 9 a.m. to 4 p.m., Saturday–Sunday, 10 a.m. to 6 p.m.;
Nov. 12–Mar. 13, Monday–Friday, 9 a.m. to 5 p.m.; May 3–Oct. 28, open until dusk
on Tuesdays and Fridays
Fee Yes

A collection of several types of gardens, of which one of the more unusual is the Lewis & Clark Native Plant Garden. Here you'll see many of the 128 plants species the explorers collected during their trek through the Northwest. The Firewise Garden shows how to landscape to protect property from wildfires. Other sections include a Celtic labyrinth, historical iris collection, water-wise gardening, and succulents. The first phase of a Children's Garden has been installed, including the "Boys in the Swing" sculpture.

IDAHO

Sawtooth Botanical Garden

Address Gimlet Rd. at Hwy. 75, Ketchum, 83340
Phone (208) 726-9358
Website www.sbgarden.org
Hours Dawn to dusk, daily
Fee No

A highlight of Sawtooth Botanical Garden is the Garden of Infinite Compassion, which honors an area visit from the Dalai Lama. The garden enables visitors to abandon worldly distractions and inner worries, thus unearthing the restorative powers of a quiet mind.

University of Idaho Charles Houston Shattuck Arboretum & Botanical Garden

Address 1200 W. Palouse River Dr., Moscow, 83843
Phone (208) 885-6250
Website www.uiweb.uidaho.edu/arboretum
Hours Daily
Fee No

Four regions are exhibited in this 61-acre arboretum: Asia, Europe, Eastern North America, and Western North America. The American Hemerocallis Society will soon designate an official daylily display garden here. Some areas have steep climbs.

Anderson Japanese Gardens

Address 318 Spring Creek Rd., Rockford, 61107
Phone (815) 229-9390
Website http://andersongardens.org
Hours May–Oct., Monday–Friday, 9 a.m. to 6 p.m.,
Saturday, 9 a.m. to 4 p.m., Sunday 10 a.m. to 4 p.m.
Fee Yes, but free on Donation Day, the third Thursday of the month

John Anderson and landscape designer Hoichi Kurisu, who designed and built the world famous Portland Japanese Garden in Oregon, have been working on this garden for more than 30 years. They were guided by the attributes of Anderson's land, from a spring-fed pond and Spring Creek. A community resource for healing, it is a regular destination for dignitaries to the area. *The Journal of Japanese Gardens* named Anderson Gardens one of the United States' best.

Chicago Botanic Garden

Address 1000 Lake Cook Rd., Glencoe, 60022
Phone (847) 835-5440; TDD (847) 835-0790
Website www.chicagobotanic.org
Hours June 5–Sept. 5, daily, 7 a.m. to 9 p.m.;
Sept. 6–June 4, daily, 8 a.m. to sunset
Fee Parking

The CBG is known for its perennial plant trials, where dozens of different cultivars are grown side-by-side and evaluated. There are 24 display gardens and four natural areas situated on nine islands surrounded by lakes. The garden maintains 2.4 million plants, most displayed in landscape settings. There is a Children's Garden, an Enabling Garden, and a Japanese Garden. Noteworthy plant collections include hardy kiwi, buckeye, dogwood, geranium, daffodils, oak, goldenrod, serviceberry, spirea, aster, willow, rose, ginkgo, Siberian iris, sedge, rush, and arborvitae.

Lincoln Memorial Garden & Nature Center

Address 2301 E. Lake Dr., Springfield, 62702
Phone (217) 529-1111
Website www.lincolnmemorialgarden.org
Hours Sunrise to sunset daily; nature center Tuesday–Saturday, 10 a.m. to 4 p.m., Sunday, 1 p.m. to 4 p.m.
Fee No

Jens Jensen designed this 100-acre site to represent the native plants and landscape that Abraham Lincoln would have known living in Kentucky, Indiana, and Illinois. It features 6 miles of trails, footbridges, a pond, eight stone council rings, and dozens of benches inscribed with Lincoln quotes.

Millennium Park

Address 201 E. Randolph St., between Michigan and
Columbus Avenues, Chicago, 60601

Phone (312) 742-1168

Website www.millenniumpark.org

Hours 6 a.m. to 11 p.m. daily

Fee No

The Lurie Garden in Millennium Park is an urban oasis emerging from a harmonious blend of symbolism, landscape design, and ecological sensitivity. Its design pays homage to Chicago's transformation from flat marshland to innovative green city, or *Urbs in Horto* (City in a Garden). Visitors find respite and inspiration in four seasons. Highlights of the garden include the dramatically lit, 15-foot-high "shoulder" hedge, a physical representation of Carl Sandburg's famous description of the "City of Big Shoulders." It encloses the garden on two sides and protects the delicate perennial garden.

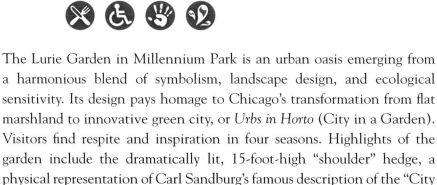

Cantigny

Address 1 S 151 Winfield Rd., Wheaton, 60189
Phone (630) 668-5161
Website www.cantigny.org
Hours Nov.–Apr., daily, 9 a.m. to sunset (closed in Jan.); May–Oct., 7 a.m. to sunset; closed Monday–Thursday in Feb.. Museum has separate hours.
Fee Parking

Cantigny is a vast, 500-acre park that encourages picnics, walking and romping on the greens, surrounded by 160,000 annuals, perennials, groundcovers, trees, and shrubs. There are formal gardens, nature walks, the Robert R McCormick Museum, and the Cantigny First Division Museum.

Garfield Park Conservatory

Address 300 N. Central Park Ave., Chicago, 60624
Phone (312) 746-5100
Website www.garfieldconservatory.org
Hours 9 a.m. to 5 p.m. daily, Wednesday, 9 a.m. to 8 p.m.
Fee No

In this complex of six greenhouses and two grand exhibition halls, visitors stroll through prehistoric ferns, step across trickling waterfalls, and experience a botanic haven where children can play, laugh, and learn. Garfield Park is an urban oasis under glass. (Special note: the Conservatory was seriously damaged by hail in 2011; call ahead.)

Illinois State University Horticultural Center

Address 1500 W. Raab Rd., Normal, 61790
Phone (309) 438-3496
Website www.horticulturecenter.illinoisstate.edu/gardens
Hours Daily
Fee No

One of the stops at the center is the Nutraceutical Garden, which combines nutrition and pharmaceuticals, or the health benefit of certain plants. There's also a Prairie Garden, All-America Selections Garden, and the Pinetum, a rare, unusual collection of cone-bearing plants.

Klehm Arboretum & Botanic Garden

Address 2715 S. Main St., Rockford, 61102
Phone (815) 963-2101
Website www.klehm.org
Hours 9 a.m. to 4 p.m. daily; summer evening hours
Fee Yes

Besides an arboretum, special areas include the Fountain Garden, Nancy Olson Children's Garden, Peony Garden, Demonstration Gardens, Hosta Garden, Prehistoric Garden, Grasses Garden, Woodland Wildflower Garden, Rhododendron & Azalea Dell, and Plant-a-Row Garden.

Morton Arboretum

Address 4100 Illinois Route 53, Lisle, 60532
Phone (630) 968-0074
Website www.mortonarb.org
Hours 7 a.m. to sunset, daily
Fee Yes

Nearly a dozen gardens are featured, including children's, maze, fragrance, four-season, rooftop, and container. The arboretum features 1,100 species of plants from the Arctic Circle to the Tropic of Cancer.

Quad City Botanical Garden

Address 2525 4th Ave., Rock Island, 61201
Phone (309) 794-0991
Website www.qcgardens.com
Hours Apr. 1–Oct. 31, Monday–Saturday, 10 a.m. to 5 p.m., Sunday, noon to 5 p.m.;
Nov. 1–Mar. 31, Monday–Saturday, 10 a.m. to 4 p.m., Sunday, noon to 4 p.m.
Fee Yes

Several themed gardens make up this special place, including Physically Challenged Garden, Rare Conifer Collection, Wildflower Prairie Garden, Garden Train Railway Exhibit, a Secret Garden, and a Perennial Garden. The conservatory features a tropical sun garden.

Hidden Hill Nursery & Sculpture Garden

Address 1011 Utica-Charlestown Rd., Utica, 47130
Phone (812) 282-0524, (812) 280-0347
Website www.hiddenhillnursery.com
Hours Apr.–Oct., weekends, or by appointment
Fee No

Hidden Hill is mini arboretum with a whimsical, eclectic collection of sculpture and unusual southern Indiana plants in landscape settings 8 miles from Louisville, Ky. Special events—music and other entertainment—are held almost every weekend April through October. Owned and operated by Jan and Bob Hill, he calls it a hobby run amok. At the center is a 150-year-old farmhouse. Over the course of 35 years, the couple turned weedy pasture land into a unique collection of gardens stocked with sculpture, plants, and joy.

Indianapolis Museum of Art

Address 4000 Michigan Rd., Indianapolis, 46208
Phone (317) 923-1331, (317) 920-2660
Website www.imamuseum.org
Hours Tuesday, Wednesday and Saturday, 11 a.m. to 5 p.m.,
Thursday and Friday, 11 a.m. to 9 p.m., Sunday, noon to 5 p.m.
Fee No, except for special exhibits, programs

Known for its art, inside and out, the IMA includes more than 150 acres of cultivated gardens, sculpture, natural areas, water features, a museum, and a historic home. Oldfields-Lilly House & Gardens is a prime example of American Country Estate living, with gardens designed by the Olmsted Brothers in the 1920s. Across the canal sits 100 Acres: The Virginia B. Fairbanks Art & Nature Park, where site-specific pieces of art adorn the natural environment. The country's ninth-oldest museum has more than 54,000 pieces of art.

New Harmony State Historic Site

Address 401 N. Arthur St., New Harmony, 47631
Phone (812) 682-4474; (800) 231-2168
Website www.usi.edu/hnh/index.php
Hours 9:30 a.m. to 5:30 p.m.
Fee Yes

The spirit that brought two nineteenth-century communal experiments still inspires visitors today. Public gardens include the Harmonist Labyrinth, Cathedral Labyrinth and Sacred Garden, David Lenz House Garden, and Church Park. Guided tours begin at the award-winning Atheneum designed by renowned architect Richard Meier.

Taltree Arboretum & Gardens

Address 450 West 100 North, Valparaiso, 46385
Phone (219) 462-0025
Website www.taltree.org
Hours Apr.–Oct., 8 a.m. to 7 p.m.; Nov.–Mar., 8 a.m. to 4 p.m.
Fee Yes

Taltree is a pleasant, 360-acre blend of formal gardens, wetlands, prairie, and woodlands with an impressive collection of conifers for the connoisseur. No doubt, the highlight is a new Railway Garden, a 2½-acre specially planted area that tells the story of American railroads. Canyons, mountains, towers, and bridges are part of the garden-scale trains' landscape, along with 500 varieties of plants, including dwarf conifers perfect for the South Lake Michigan Region and other Midwestern gardens.

Foellinger-Freimann Botanical Conservatory

Address 1100 S. Calhoun St., Fort Wayne, 46802
Phone (260) 427-6440
Website www.botanicalconservatory.org
Hours Tuesday–Saturday, 10 a.m. to 5 p.m., Thursday, 10 a.m. to 8 p.m., Sunday, noon to 4 p.m.
Fee Yes

Right in the heart of downtown Fort Wayne sits an oasis of glass and gardens inside and out. The 25,000-square-foot conservatory protects 1,200 plants, including 72 types of cacti. Outdoors, rhododendrons, trees, shrubs, ornamental grasses, perennials, and annuals decorate the scene.

Garfield Park Sunken Garden & Conservatory

Address 2505 Conservatory Dr., Indianapolis, 46203
Phone (317) 327-7184
Website www.garfieldgardensconservatory.org
Hours Conservatory, Monday–Saturday, 10 a.m. to 5 p.m., Sunday, 1 p.m. to 5 p.m.; Sunken Garden Apr. 23–Oct. 11, 10 a.m. to 9 p.m.; Oct. 12–Apr. 22, 10 a.m. to 5 p.m.
Fee Yes, for conservatory and special programs. Gardens are free.

Three fountains form the centerpiece at the city's oldest park, where seasonal plants are changed three times a year. The conservatory has 800 orchid species, cacao and banana trees, finches, and fish flourishing amid lush tropical plants. You will also find a children's garden, butterfly show, and seasonally, holiday trains, lights, and poinsettias.

Gene Stratton-Porter State Historic Site

Address 1205 Pleasant Point, Rome City, 46784
  Phone (260) 854-3790
Website www.genestratton-porter.com
    Hours Grounds, dawn to dusk year-round; cabin, Apr. 1–Dec. 1, Tuesday–Saturday,
        10 a.m. to 5 p.m., Sunday, 1 p.m. to 5 p.m.; Dec. 2–Mar. 31, by appointment.
      Fee Yes

The author of *The Girl of the Limberlost*, *Freckles*, and *Song of the Cardinal*, planted gardens of Indiana wildflowers, many of them rescued from agriculture drainage sites and other development. Stratton-Porter's second Indiana home is nestled on Sylvan Lake. The Cabin in the Wildflowers retains its 1917 character.

Hayes Regional Arboretum

Address 801 Elks Rd., Richmond, 47374
  Phone (765) 962-3745
Website www.hayesarboretum.org
    Hours Mar.–Oct., Tuesday–Saturday, 9 a.m. to 5 p.m.; Nov.–Feb., open for special events and
        scheduled programs
      Fee No

Three percent of Indiana's old growth forest can be found at the Hayes, which also is known for its rock and fossil collections, Indian mounds, wetlands, ponds, and fields along with unusual trees on the 446 acres. The Nature Center has interpretive programs about tree history and other exhibits.

Hill Memorial Rose Garden

Address 2500 National Rd. East (U.S. 40), Richmond, 47374
Phone (765) 962-1511
Website www.waynet.org/nonprofit/rosegarden
Hours Dawn to dusk
Fee No

Located in Glen Miller Park, the Hill Rose Garden was founded in 1937 and features a Victorian gazebo and German Friendship Garden. It has been designated an All-American Rose Society Display Destination. Peak bloom time is June and September. You won't want to miss it.

Hilltop Garden & Nature Center

Address 2367 E. 10th St., Bloomington, 47408
Phone (812) 855-8808
Website www.iub.edu/~hilltop
Hours Monday–Friday, 9 a.m. to 4 p.m. , Saturday, 11 a.m. to 4 p.m.
Fee No

Located on the campus of Indiana University, Hilltop has one of the oldest children's gardening programs in the country. Each summer, children grow food or flowers in their own beds at Hilltop. The nature center serves as a research and meeting resource for various plant groups.

Lanier Mansion State Historic Site

Address 601 W. First St., Madison, 47250

Phone (812) 265-3526

Website www.indianamuseum.org/sites/lani

Hours 9 a.m. to 5 p.m. daily

Fee Yes

The James Lanier Mansion, a prime example of Greek Revival architecture, is the crown jewel of Madison's historic district. The south portico overlooks the Ohio River. Below the house, formal gardens developed after the Civil War have been recreated with plant varieties authentic to the period.

Medicinal Plant Garden

Address 3045 W. Vermont St., Indianapolis, 46222

Phone (317) 635-7329

Website www.imhm.org

Hours Wednesday–Saturday, 10 a.m. to 4 p.m.; June–Sept., Saturdays at 11 a.m., free guided tours

Fee No

The garden at the Indiana Medical History Museum was created and is maintained by Marion County Master Gardeners. More than 90 medicinal plants are in the garden, each accompanied by signage stating its origin, the parts that have medicinal uses, and what some of those uses were.

INDIANA

Minnetrista Center

Address 1200 N. Minnetrista Parkway, Muncie, 47303
Phone (765) 282-4848, (800) 428-5887
Website www.minnetrista.net
Hours Monday–Saturday, 9 a.m. to 5:30 p.m., Sunday, 11 a.m. to 5:30 p.m.
Fee Yes, for exhibits

Minnetrista was the name of the F.C. Ball home that was at this site; it's now a cultural, nature, and landscape center. Oakhurst Gardens, the estate of George Ball, contains a renovated 1895 home and six acres of gardens.

Purdue University Horticulture Gardens

Address 1165 Horticulture Bldg., Marstellar St. at Agricultural Mall, West Lafayette, 47907
Phone (765) 494-1296
Website www.hort.purdue.edu/ext/hort_gardens.html
Hours Dawn to dusk
Fee No

Visitors learn about new plants and gardening techniques at this half-acre garden filled with hundreds of perennials, annuals, and vegetables. Vistiors can see how cultivars perform in side-by-side plantings featuring many new cultivars. Special collections include peonies, daylilies, hostas, spring-flowering bulbs, and ornamental grasses.

T.C. Steele Home State Historic Site

Address 4220 T.C. Steel Rd., Nashville, 47448
Phone (812) 988-2785
Website www.tcsteele.org
Hours Tuesday–Saturday, 9 a.m. to 5 p.m., Sunday, 1 p.m.–5 p.m.
Fee Yes, for building tours, free for grounds

This site includes the last home and studio of Indiana artist T.C. Steele and his wife, Selma. The 211 acres of wooded hills and ravines inspired the artist to paint some of his most famous works. The gardens are filled with daffodils and peonies in spring.

Warsaw Biblical Gardens

Address Canal Street and Ind. 15, Warsaw, 46580
Phone (574) 267-6419
Website www.warsawbiblicalgardens.org
Hours May 15–Sept. 15, dawn to dusk
Fee Yes, for tours, grounds free

Included in the three-quarter-acre site are the Forest, Brook, Meadow, Desert, Crop, and Herb gardens, the Grape Arbor, and the Gathering site. In certain instances where plants of the exact genus were either not available or would not survive, the gardens have substituted species or cultivars of the same genus.

Wellfield Botanic Gardens

Address 1000 N. Main St., Elkhart, 46514
Phone (574) 266-2006
Website www.wellfieldgardens.org
Hours 7 a.m. to 6 p.m. daily
Fee No

Wellfield Botanic Gardens accepts as truth that mankind is inseparable from nature. The gardens provide a shared natural and man-made environment of unique beauty that attracts, inspires, and educates in a setting dedicated to the celebration of nature and art.

White River Gardens/Indianapolis Zoo

Address 1200 W. Washington St., Indianapolis, 46222
Phone (317) 630-2001
Website www.indyzoo.com
Hours Monday–Thursday, 9 a.m. to 5 p.m., Friday–Sunday, 9 a.m. to 7 p.m.
Fee Yes

The stunningly beautiful 3.3-acre landmark botanical attraction combines the best of gardening ideas, plant information, and inspirational design. With hundreds of plant varieties on display plus entertaining special exhibits throughout the year, the gardens allow visitors to enjoy and learn about the bounty of the natural world.

Reiman Gardens

Address 1407 University Blvd., Ames, 50014
Phone (515) 294-2710
Website www.reimangardens.iastate.edu
Hours Memorial Day to Labor Day, 9 a.m. to 6 p.m.; other times,
9 a.m. to 4:30 p.m.
Fee Yes

Part of Iowa State University, Reiman has a new rose garden that was designed and planted and is maintained in a sustainable manner. Its overall goal is to give visitors ideas they can use at home and that demonstrate the low- or no-use of chemical products. The Patty Jischke Children's Garden features a maze, water play, and a hideout. In spring, more than 20,000 bulbs bloom along with perennials, annuals, shrubs, and trees. Dunlap Courtyard offers sweeping views of the gardens under the shade of catalpa trees.

Seed Savers Exchange Heritage Farm

Address 3094 N. Winn Rd., Decorah, 52101
Phone (563) 382-5990
Website www.seedsavers.org
Hours Apr.–Oct., 9 a.m. to 5 p.m. weekdays,
10 am. to 5 p.m. weekends.
Fee No

Founded in 1975, Seed Savers Exchange is a not-for-profit membership organization dedicated to saving and sharing North America's diverse, yet threatened, garden heritage. The 890-acre Heritage Farm is where these heirloom plants are grown and propagated. The farm is ringed by hiking trails that go to the Preservation Garden, Historic Orchard, and beside pastures of rare, wild white Park cattle, a breed believed to date before Christ and which are described in Celtic yore. Amish carpenters built a meeting center and the recently completed Lillian Goldman Visitors Center.

Bickelhaupt Arboretum

Address 340 S. 14th St., Clinton, 52732
Phone (563) 242-4771
Website www.bick-arb.org
Hours Dawn to dusk, daily
Fee No

This is a 14-acre outdoor museum of select labeled trees, shrubs, groundcovers, perennials, and annual flowers developed by Robert and Frances Bickelhaupt and their private foundation. Rose, butterfly, country, herb, conifer, native prairie, shade tree, and wildflower gardens set the scene.

Brenton Arboretum

Address 25141 260th St., Dallas Center, 50063
Phone (515) 992-4211
Website www.thebrentonarboretum.org
Hours Tuesday–Sunday, 9 a.m. to sunset
Fee No

The 140-acre Brenton Arboretum has more than 5 miles of walking trails that follow the edges of lakes and ponds. You'll discover 2,600 trees and shrubs representing 175 species, all identified. Their love of trees prompted the Brenton family to found the arboretum.

Cedar Valley Arboretum & Botanic Gardens

Address 1927 E. Orange Rd., Waterloo, 50701
Phone (319) 226-4966
Website www.cedarvalleyarboretum.org
Hours Apr.–Oct., dawn to dusk
Fee No

On 74 acres near Hawkeye Community College sits the Silos & Smokestacks National Heritage Area and several gardens, walking paths, and an education center. Themed gardens include an Enabling Garden, Children's Garden, Display Garden, Community Garden, Rose Garden, and a labyrinth.

Dubuque Arboretum & Botanical Gardens

Address 3800 Arboretum Dr., Dubuque, 52001
Phone (563) 556-2100
Website www.dubuquearboretum.com
Hours May 1–Oct. 31, 7 a.m. to dusk daily; Nov. 1–May 1, 10 a.m. to 3 p.m.;
closed Saturday and Sunday.
Fee No

Free concerts on summer Sundays is just one of the fun things about this arboretum and botanical garden, the largest one operated solely by volunteers. It's the country's largest public hosta garden with 1,300 plants representing 700 varieties.

Iowa Arboretum

Address 1875 Peach St., Madrid, 50156
Phone (515) 795-3216
Website www.iowaarboretum.org
Hours Sunrise to sunset daily
Fee No

Follow the trails to learn about 19 different plant collections are grouped by their uses. There are ravines, streams, overlooks, and collections of nut trees, a peony labyrinth, and the Stout Medal Daylilies display.

Vander Veer Botanical Park

Address 214 W. Central Park, Davenport, 52803
Phone (563) 326-7812
Website www.cityofdavenportiowa.com/department/division.php?fDD=21-223
Hours Park, sunrise to one-half hour past sunset daily; Conservatory, Tuesday–Saturday, 10 a.m. to 4 p.m., free on Tuesday.
Fee Yes, for conservatory, park is free

The Grand Allée leads to the Stone Fountain with its dancing, billowing water and changing lights. A popular place for walking, the 33-acre park, established in 1885, has a conservatory and nineteenth-century German-style formal gardens. There's a playground and lagoon for kids.

Botanica, The Wichita Gardens

Address 701 Amidon, Wichita, 67203
Phone (316) 264-0448
Website www.botanica.org
Hours Monday–Saturday, 9 a.m. to 5 p.m.; Apr.–Oct., Sunday,
1 p.m. to 5 p.m.; Tuesday–Thursday, 9 a.m. to 8 p.m.
Fee Yes

Twenty-four themed gardens have been created since the 9.5-acre garden opened in the mid-1980s. The Downing Children's Garden opened in 2011 and features a farm with raised beds, a giant tree and tree house, a musical maze, monster trees, and a pond to hop across. The Woodland Bird Garden opened in 2011 and is a wildlife friendly environment. At least 20 sculptures are placed throughout the garden. There's also a sensory garden, a three-season perennial border, and a greenhouse with tropical and exotic plants.

Dyck Arboretum of the Plains

Address 177 W. Hickory St., Hesston, 67062

Phone (620) 327-8127

Website www.dyckarboretum.org

Hours Monday–Friday, 9 a.m. to 4 p.m.; May 1–Oct. 15, Saturday and Sunday, 1 p.m. to 4 p.m.

Fee Yes

Operated by Hesston College, this 13-acre arboretum and garden offers four seasons of natural beauty with a focus on prairie plants, including wildflowers, trees, and shrubs, and tall and short grasses. Plants are labeled and arranged to give visitors take-home ideas. The Visitor and Education Center with its stone and wood exterior was designed to convey an image of the ridge and valley topography reminiscent of the Flint Hills of Kansas.

Overland Park Arboretum and Botanical Gardens

Address 8909 W. 179th St., Overland Park, 66013
  Phone (913) 685-3604
Website www.opkansas.org
    Hours Apr. 10–Sept. 30, 8 a.m. to 7:30 p.m.; Oct. 1–Apr. 9, 8 a.m. to 5 p.m.
      Fee No

The 300-acre Overland Park Arboretum & Botanical Gardens was founded to keep the city at the forefront of environmental and ecological issues. About 85 percent of the land is dedicated to the preservation and restoration of 8 natural ecosystems.

Reinisch Rose Garden and Doran Rock Garden

Address 685 SW Gage Blvd., Topeka, 66606 (Reinisch Rose Garden)
        4320 SW 10th St., Topeka, 66604 (Doran Rock Garden)
  Phone (785) 272-5900
Website www.topeka.org/parksrec/gage_park.shtml
  Hours Daily
      Fee No

The 160-acre Gage Park encompasses both of these gardens. It has one of about two dozen test gardens for the All-America Rose Selections. Reinisch features more than 400 varieties and 2,300 plants, and annuals fill the Doran Rock Garden. Nearby is the Von Rohr Victorian Gardens, which surround a large pond.

Sedgwick County Extension Arboretum

Address 7001 W. 21st St., Wichita, 67205
Phone (316) 660-0100
Website www.sedgwick.ksu.edu
Hours Daily
Fee No

The grounds are planted and maintained by Sedgwick County Extension Master Gardeners. Included in the arboretum is a raised bed demonstration garden of vegetables and flowers, container gardens, rose gardens, a nature trail, and ornamental grasses. All plants are labeled.

Ward-Meade Park Botanic Gardens

Address 124 N. Fillmore, Topeka, 66606
Phone (785) 368-3888
Website www.topeka.org/parksrec/wardmeade_gardens.shtml
Hours Varied
Fee Yes

Every season brings a different beauty to the $2^1/2$ acres of botanical gardens at Old Prairie Town at Ward-Meade Historic Site. A special feature of the gardens is Anna's Place, a Victorian Reading Garden.

Yew Dell Gardens

Address 6220 Old LaGrange Rd., Crestwood, 40014
Phone (502) 241-4788
Website www.yewdellgardens.org
Hours Apr.–Nov., Monday–Saturday, 10 a.m. to 4 p.m., Sunday,
noon to 4 p.m.; Dec.–Mar., Monday–Friday, 10 a.m. to 4 p.m.
Fee No

A formal topiary garden, traditional English walled garden, and a signature Serpentine Garden was the backdrop for the development of this commercial nursery and private estate, which opened to the public in 2005. The late owners, Theodore and Martha Lee Klein, displayed more than a thousand unusual specimen trees and shrubs for evaluation. The property includes an arboretum, a secret garden flanked by a holly allée, hellebores, and hardy gingers. A lovely focal point is a Cotswolds-style fieldstone house and an Adrian Bloom–designed garden.

Bernheim Arboretum and Research Forest

Address 2499 Old State Hwy 245, Clermont, 40110
Phone (502) 955-8512
Website www.bernheim.org
Hours 7 a.m. to sunset, daily
Fee Free weekdays, auto fee on weekends

Bernheim has 35 miles of hiking trails that loop through knobs and valleys, and along ridges and hollows. Bicycling also is allowed. The award-winning visitor center is built like a tree and features green building techniques, including carbon sequestration, shade, comfort and water protection.

Boone County Arboretum

Address 9190 Camp Ernst Rd., Union, 41091
Phone (859) 384-4999
Website www.bcarboretum.org
Hours Dawn to dusk
Fee No

Located in a recreation park in northern Kentucky, the arboretum is a living museum of 3,000 trees and shrubs. It has a 2-mile hiking trail, a children's garden, and a wildlife viewing area. The arboretum is in Central Park.

State Botanical Garden of Kentucky

Address 500 Alumni Dr., Lexington, 40503
Phone (859) 257-6955
Website www.ca.uky.edu/arboretum/
Hours Dawn to dusk, daily
Fee No, except for Children's Garden

Visitors stroll through gardens of roses, fragrance, perennials, annuals, herbs, vegetables, groundcovers, home fruit and nut plants, and other displays. There's a fee for the Children's Garden and plans for a new one. The arboretum's 100 acres boast year-round color and plant interest.

Western Kentucky Botanical Gardens

Address 25 Carter Rd., Owensboro, 42301
Phone (270) 852-8925
Website www.wkbg.org
Hours Mar.–Nov. 14, daily, 9 a.m. to 3 p.m.; Nov. 14–Feb., Monday–Friday, 9 a.m. to 3 p.m.
Fee Yes

Among the gardens is the Mary Takahashi Japanese Memorial Garden, which is dedicated to the well-known Ikebana designer and author. For the kids, there's the Moonlit Children's Garden, which includes a gourd teepee and a maze of 'China Girl' hollies.

American Rose Center

Address 8877 Jefferson Paige Rd., Shreveport, 71119
Phone (318) 938-5534; (800) 637-6534
Website www.ars.org
Hours Apr.–Oct., Monday–Saturday, 9 a.m. to 5 p.m.,
Sunday, 1 p.m. to 5 p.m.
Fee Yes

The Gardens of the American Rose Center, located on a 118-acre wooded tract, is home to the national headquarters of the American Rose Society. It is the nation's largest park dedicated to roses. The gardens were dedicated in 1974 when the American Rose Society headquarters moved to Shreveport, Louisiana, from Columbus, Ohio. Today, the American Rose Center features more than 65 individual rose gardens and 20,000 rosebushes, with a variety of companion plants, sculptures, and fountains.

LOUISIANA

Longue Vue House & Gardens

Address 7 Bamboo Rd., New Orleans, 70124
Phone (504) 488-5488
Website www.longuevue.com/
Hours Tuesday–Saturday, 10 a.m. to 5 p.m., Sunday, 1 p.m. to 5 p.m.
Fee Yes

Known for its famous allée of southern live oaks, the gardens also include boxwood parterres, a yellow garden, a Spanish court, azalea walk, goldfish pond, a Portuguese-inspired canal garden, a walled garden, and a wild garden. Original works of twentieth-century art adorns the Classical Revival home, including Kandinsky, Picasso, Gabo, Michel, Laurens, Agam, Arp, Hepworth, and Soto. Damaged by Hurricane Katrina, the gardens have been restored with the help of volunteers from all over the United States.

Afton Villa and Gardens

Address 9047 Hwy. 61, St. Francisville, 70775
Phone (225) 721-2269 or (225) 635-6773
Website www.aftonvilla.com
Hours Mar. 1–June 20 and Oct. 1–Dec. 1, daily, 9 a.m. to 4:30 p.m.
Fee Yes

Only the 250 acres of gardens remain on this historic property since the antebellum mansion burned in 1963. The gardens are adorned with reproduction Greek and Roman statues and other pieces of art reflective of old Southern living.

Biedenharn Museum & Gardens

Address 2006 Riverside Dr., Monroe, 71201
Phone (318) 387-5281 or (800) 362-0983
Website www.bmuseum.org
Hours Tuesday–Saturday, 10 a.m. to 5 p.m.
Fee Yes

The Biedenharn Museum & Gardens features a historic home, formal garden, Bible Museum, and Coke Museum. ELsong Garden is a beautifully walled English garden. A stunning Wagnerian fountain is located on the north end of the Ballet Lawn.

Burden Horticulture Society

Address 4560 Essen Lane, Baton Rouge, 70809
Phone (225) 763-3990
Website www.burdenhorticulturesociety.com
Hours 8 a.m. to 5 p.m. daily
Fee No

The Burden Center is a collection of gardens, trails, sculpture, and other sites of horticultural interest that is associated with Louisiana State University and managed by the horticultural society. Highlights are the Camellia Gardens and the Ginger Gardens.

Hilltop Arboretum

Address 11855 Highland Rd., Baton Rouge, 70810
Phone (225) 767-6916
Website www.hilltop.lsu.edu/hilltop/hilltop.nsf
Hours Daylight hours
Fee No

Cross the old footbridge overlooking a 20-foot-deep ravine and wander into the tranquil cathedral of trees. Discover the bamboo grove, and walk through a meadow where tall grasses and colorful autumn wildflowers shimmer in the bright Louisiana sunlight. The Hilltop Arboretum is part of Louisiana State University.

Coastal Maine Botanical Gardens

Address 132 Botanical Gardens Dr., Boothbay, 04537
Phone (207) 633-4333
Website www.mainegardens.org
Hours 9 a.m. to 5 p.m. daily
Fee Yes, free from Dec.–Mar.

The shoreline is visible throughout the seasons along hiking trails. Kids will enjoy the Bibby and Harold Alfond Children's Garden, with whale spray, dragon growls, and a bronze bear on the move. Kids can climb through boats, find their way through a maze, and greet a Miss Rumphium topiary. Adjacent to the Kitchen Garden Café is a Burpee Kitchen Garden with a granite fountain. The Cleaver Event Lawn & Garden features large borders of perennials, shrubs, and other plants.

Asticou Azalea Garden

Address Asticou Way, Seal Harbor and Peabody Dr., Mount Desert, 04662
Phone (207) 276-3727
Website www.gardenpreserve.org
Hours May–Oct., daylight
Fee No

Designed by Charles K. Savage, Asticou Azalea Garden was developed to salvage Beatrix Farrand's plants from her nearby Reef Point estate. It has traditional Japanese design features with plants that thrive in coastal Maine. Start at the Mount Desert Land & Garden preserve.

Merryspring Nature Center

Address 30 Conway Rd., Camden, 04843
Phone (207) 236-2239
Website www.merryspring.org
Hours Dawn to dusk, daily
Fee No

This is a 66-acre public garden where it's alright to collect a few seeds or ask for plant cuttings. Natural trails and gardens include annuals, roses, a rock garden, hostas, herbs, birds and butterfly garden, daylilies, and a children's garden. There's also a greenhouse and arboretum.

Thuya Garden, Northeast Harbor

Address Peabody Dr., Mount Desert, 04662
Phone (207) 276-3727
Website www.gardenpreserve.org
Hours Late May to mid-Oct., daily, 7 a.m. to 7 p.m.
Fee No

The 140-acre preserve includes Thuya Garden, Thuya Lodge, Asticou Terraces, and Asticou Landing. Lookouts traverse the hillside from the eastern shore of Northeast Harbor to Thuya Lodge. The lodge was named for the area's abundant stands of northern white cedar, *Thuya occidentalis*, which is usually spelled *Thuja*.

Wild Gardens of Acadia

Address Route 233, McFarland Hill, Bar Harbor, 04609
Phone (207) 288-3338
Website www.nps.gov/acad/planyourvisit/wildgardens.htm
Hours Daily
Fee Yes

Twelve of Acadia's plant communities are represented here: mixed woods, roadside, meadow, mountain, heath, seaside, brookside, bird thicket, coniferous woods, bog, marsh, and pond. All can be found at Wild Gardens on less than an acre of Mount Desert Island's natural habitat in Acadia National Park.

Brookside Gardens

Address 1800 Glenallan Ave., Wheaton, 20902
Phone (301) 962-1400
Website www.montgomeryparks.org/brookside
Hours Sunrise to sunset
Fee No

Brookside Gardens is Montgomery County's incomparable, award-winning 50-acre public display garden situated within Wheaton Regional Park. Included are several distinct areas: Aquatic Garden, Azalea Garden, Butterfly Garden, Children's Garden, Rose Garden, Japanese Style Garden, Trial Garden, Rain Garden, and the Woodland Walk. The Formal Gardens area includes a Perennial Garden, Yew Garden, the Maple Terrace, and Fragrance Garden. Brookside Gardens also features two conservatories for year-round enjoyment.

Druid Hill Park Conservatory

Address 2600 Madison Ave., Baltimore, 21217
Phone (410) 396-6106
Website www.druidhillpark.org
Hours Tuesday–Sunday, 10 a.m. to 4 p.m.
Fee No

Begun in 1880, Druid Hill Park ranks with Central Park in New York and Fairmount Park in Philadelphia as the United States' oldest public, landscaped parks. Druid Hill is home to the Maryland Zoo and the Rawlings Conservatory, with its Palm House and Orchid Room, and the outdoor botanic garden. The Jones Falls Trail is for bicycling or hiking around Druid Hill Lake. Druid Hill Lake was built in 1863 and remains one of the largest earth-dammed lakes in the United States.

William Paca Gardens

Address 186 Prince George St., Annapolis, 21401
Phone (410) 990-4543
Website www.annapolis.org
Hours Monday–Saturday, 10 a.m. to 5 p.m., Sunday, noon to 5 p.m.
Fee Yes

The two-acre oasis of natural beauty and artful elegance, which rests in the heart of historic Annapolis, has been restored to its original splendor. Multi-tier terraces define the garden. The upper terrace provides a space for entertaining and viewing the garden terrain. On the middle terrace, precise geometric parterres show off three seasons of colorful blooms, heirloom roses, and period-style topiary. The lower terraces feature a fish-shaped pond whose bridge leads to a two-story summer house, plus serpentine paths through lush lawns and beds of native plants.

Adkins Arboretum

Address 12610 Eveland Rd., Ridgely, 21660
Phone (410) 634-2847
Website www.adkinsarboretum.org
Hours 10 a.m. to 4 p.m. daily
Fee Yes

Adkins Arboretum is a 400-acre preserve on Maryland's Eastern Shore whose purpose is to promote the appreciation and conservation of the region's native plants. Five miles of paths meander along streams, through meadows, and beside native plant gardens. The site features over 600 species of native shrubs, trees, wildflowers, and grasses.

Annmarie Sculpture Garden

Address 13480 Dowell Rd., Solomons, 20629
Phone (410) 326-4640
Website www.annmariegarden.org
Hours Sculpture Garden, 9 a.m. to 5 p.m. daily
Fee Yes

Located where the Patuxent River meets Chesapeake Bay, the 30-acre sculpture garden features a ¼-mile walking path that meanders through the woods past permanent and loaned sculpture. Thirty works are on loan from the Smithsonian Institution and the National Gallery of Art. There are plans to create a Children's Discovery Garden and Nature Trail; check their website for updates.

Cylburn Garden Center

Address 4915 Greenspring Ave., Baltimore, 21209
Phone (410) 367-2217
Website www.cylburnassociation.org
Hours Tuesday–Saturday, 8 a.m. to 8 p.m.
Fee No

Gardens surround this post–Civil War mansion, built of gneiss mined from the Tyson family's quarries. The fireplaces, inlaid floors, mosaics, tapestries and ornate plasterwork have been preserved. Volunteers designed the trails and gardens and have developed Cylburn as a center for environmental education and horticulture.

Hampton National Historic Site

Address 535 Hampton Lane, Towson, 21286
Phone 410-823-1309
Website www.historichampton.org
Hours 9 a.m. to 6 p.m. daily
Fee No

Historic Hampton Mansion is noted for its many original outbuildings. In addition to the mansion are the original ice house and two-story stone stable, plus a reconstructed orangery. Historic trees include catalpas dating to colonial times, a cedar of Lebanon planted in 1830, and a saucer magnolia from the Marquis de Lafayette. History is literally living here.

Historic London Town and Gardens

Address 839 Londontown Rd., Edgewater, 21037
Phone (410) 222-1919
Website www.historiclondontown.org
Hours Apr.–Dec., Wednesday–Saturday, 10 a.m. to 4:30 p.m., Sunday, noon to 4:30 p.m.; Jan.–Feb., 10 a.m. to 4 p.m., reduced admission
Fee Yes

Explore the historic area, which includes the circa 1760 William Brown House and ongoing archaeological investigations in search of the "lost town" of London. A Woodland Garden of native and exotic plants lines a 1-mile trail to the seasonal Ornamental Gardens that overlook the scenic South River.

Ladew Topiary Garden

Address 3535 Jarrettsville Pike, Monkton, 21111
Phone (410) 557-9466
Website www.ladewgardens.com
Hours Late Mar.–Oct. 31, Monday–Friday, 10 a.m. to 4 p.m., Saturday and Sunday, 10:30 a.m. to 5 p.m.
Fee Yes

Ladew's 22 acres are filled with all types of topiary, including a hunt—complete with dogs, horses, riders, and foxes—a Chinese water scene, and swans and other animals. Ladew created 15 garden "rooms," each with a monoculture, monochromatic color scheme, or a single theme.

Arnold Arboretum

Address 125 Arborway, Boston, 02130
Phone (617) 524-1718
Website www.arboretum.harvard.edu
Hours Sunrise to sunset, daily
Fee No

The oldest arboretum in the United States, the Arnold is owned and managed by Harvard. Since its beginning in 1872, the arboretum has collected plants from Asia and North America. Visitors can stroll through a terraced garden of sun-loving vines—a group of plants that rarely get displayed in gardens. Search for the "tree of the month," and participate in other family activities. For about five weeks every spring, the arboretum is filled with the scent of nearly 400 lilacs, one of the plants in its collection.

Naumkeag

Address 5 Prospect Hill Rd., Stockbridge, 01238
Phone (413) 298-3239
Website www.gardensoftheberkshires.org/Naumkeag.htm
Hours Late May to Columbus Day, 10 a.m. to 5 p.m. daily
Fee

Representative of the Gilded Age, Naumkeag (designed by Stanford White) is noted for its iconic, white birch lined, blue Art Deco steps designed by noted landscape architect Fletcher Steele. Steele's style was almost lyrical, and he became increasingly interested in designing landscapes that were artistic rather than formulaic. All of the 8 acres of gardens are beautifully created, including the Afternoon Garden, Tree Peony Terrace, Rose Garden, Evergreen Garden, and Chinese Garden. *Naumkeag* is what Native Americans called Salem. The Choate family retreated to the 44-room home from April through November. The home is also on display.

MASSACHUSSETTS

Berkshire Botanical Garden

Address W. Stockbridge Rd., Rt. 102 & 183, Stockbridge, 01266
Phone (413) 298-3926
Website www.berkshirebotanical.org
Hours May 1 to Columbus Day, 9 a.m. to 5 p.m. daily
Fee Yes

Now a collection of more than 3,000 species, this 15-acre garden displays plants that thrive in the Berkshires in an informal country setting. This is one of the United States' oldest botanical gardens and serves as an inspirational resource for the community.

Botanic Garden of Smith College

Address 16 College Lane, Northampton, 01060
Phone (413) 585-2740
Website www.smith.edu/garden
Hours Daily
Fee No

The firm Olmsted, Olmsted and Eliot designed Smith College's comprehensive landscape plan in 1893 with all of the firm's famous design elements: curved drives, walkways that lead to gardens, and open vistas. Of special interest is a systematics garden, where plants are arranged by their evolutionary relationships to one another. All together, there are about 10,000 plants of 6,600 different kinds.

Chesterwood

Address 4 Williamsville Rd., Stockbridge, 01266
Phone (413) 298-3579
Website www.chesterwood.org
Hours May 29– mid-Oct., daily; May 1–28 and the last three weekends in Oct., weekends, 10 a.m. to 5 p.m.
Fee Yes

This is the home and garden of artist Daniel Chester French, who created the Abraham Lincoln sculpture in the Lincoln Memorial. There's usually a major exhibition of contemporary sculpture through the summer in the gardens.

Heritage Museum & Gardens

Address 67 Grove St., Sandwich, 02563
Phone (508) 888-3300
Website www.heritagemuseumsandgardens.org
Hours May 1–Oct. 31, 10 a.m. to 5 p.m. daily
Fee Yes

Four museums—J.K. Lilly III Antique Automobile Museum, American History Museum, Art Museum, and Old East Windmill—share the grounds with 100 acres of labeled trees and shrubs, designed gardens, beautiful flowers, and sweeping lawns and plants with four seasons of interest.

Massachusetts Horticultural Society

Address 900 Washington St. (Rt. 16), Wellesley, 02482
Phone (617) 933-4900
Website www.masshort.org
Hours 8 a.m. to dusk
Fee Yes

In this hands-on education center, visitors can tour an All-America Selections Garden, Bressingham Garden, Italianate Garden, and the Goddess Garden. Of special interest, early viewers of *The Victory Garden* on PBS will appreciate the James Crockett Memorial Garden.

New England Wild Flower Society

Address 180 Hemenway Rd., Framingham, 01701
Phone (508) 877-7630, TTY (508) 877-6553
Website www.newenglandwild.org
Hours Apr. 15–July 4, Tuesday–Sunday, 9 a.m.–5 p.m., Thursday, 8 a.m. to 8 p.m.;
July 5–Oct. 31, Tuesday–Sunday, 9 a.m.–5 p.m.
Fee Yes

At the headquarters, the Garden in the Wood and botanic garden, with walking paths and trails, is the largest collection of native plants species in New England. The society has several other sites in the area that are open for visitors.

Polly Hill Arboretum

Address 795 State Rd., West Tisbury, 02575
Phone (508) 693-9426
Website www.pollyhillarboretum.org
Hours Sunrise to sunset, daily
Fee Yes

The 40-acre arboretum on Martha's Vineyard holds a lovely collection of stewartia, magnolias, witch hazels, hollies, camellias, conifers, and hornbeams with a scenic dogwood boulevard. Meadows and woodlands have been preserved to ensure a diverse habitat. An administrative building dates to the late 1600s.

Stanley Park

Address 400 Western Ave., Westfield, 01085
Phone (413) 568-9312
Website www.stanleypark.org
Hours 7 a.m. to dusk, daily, from the first Saturday in May to the last Sunday in Nov.
Fee No

The American Wildflower Society Display Garden is at its peak in early May in the Woodland Wildflower Garden at this 300-acre park. There's also a bog garden, herb garden, rhododendron display garden, rose garden, and a Japanese garden. A 5-acre arboretum features a 30-foot-tall fountain.

MASSACHUSSETTS

Tower Hill Botanic Garden

Address 11 French Dr., Boylston, 01505
Phone (508) 869-6111
Website www.towerhillbg.org
Hours May– Sept., Tuesday–Sunday, 9 a.m. to 5 p.m., open until 8 p.m. on Wednesday
Fee Yes

Two greenhouses flank a new Winter Garden, which showcases plants that offer seasonal interest, such as berries or colorful bark. Limonaia, a special house for lemons and other tropical fruits, opened in 2010 on the 132-acre site.

Vale, the Lyman Estate

Address 185 Lyman St., Waltham, 02452
Phone (781) 891-4882
Website www.historicnewengland.org
Hours Greenhouse, Dec. 15–July 15, Wednesday–Sunday;
July 16–Dec. 14, Wednesday–Saturday, 9:30 a.m. to 4 p.m.
Fee No for grounds

What is believed to be the United States' oldest greenhouse sits on this 37-acre estate. Considered a fine example of the American Country Estate, this 24-room Federalist-style mansion is open for tours for a fee by reservation only.

Fernwood Botanical Garden & Nature Preserve

Address 13988 Range Line Rd., Niles, 49120
Phone (269) 695-6491
Website www.fernwoodbotanical.org
Hours Nov.–Apr., Tuesday–Saturday, 10 a.m. to 5 p.m.,
Sunday, noon to 5 p.m.; May–Oct., Tuesday–Saturday,
10 a.m. to 6 p.m., Sunday, noon to 6 p.m.
Fee Yes

Fernwood is situated on the St. Joseph River near Buchanan in SW Michigan's wine country. The garden is 90 minutes from Chicago, and 20 minutes to Lake Michigan's shore. Fernwood comprises 105 acres of cultivated gardens and natural areas. Features include a fern conservatory, art gallery, nature center, library, café, and garden and gift shops. The garden offers a new outdoor sculpture exhibition, herb garden, arboretum, prairie, fern and hosta collections, rock garden, railway garden, boxwood garden, perennial cottage border, Japanese garden, and other special features. Fernwood offers classes, lectures, concerts, festivals, art shows, trips and tours, summer youth camps, and more.

Frederik Meijer Gardens & Sculpture Park

Address 1000 E. Beltline Ave., N.E., Grand Rapids, 49525
Phone (888) 957-1580
Website www.meijergardens.org
Hours Monday, Wednesday–Saturday, 9 a.m. to 5 p.m.,
Tuesday, 9 a.m. to 9 p.m., Sunday, 11 a.m. to 5 p.m.
Fee Yes

This 132-acre venue is landscaping and art on a grand scale, with sculpture and gardens that fully complement one another. Artists, including Rodin, Moore, Oldenburg, DiSuervo, and others, provide an incredible collection of art all in one place. Listed on several "must see" museum lists, the four-season gardens were designed by James van Sweden of the United States and British designer Penelope Hobhouse. The Wege Nature Trail is a paved pathway through a forest and connects to Frey Boardwalk, which leads to a natural wetland.

Michigan 4-H Children's Garden

Address Bogue St., Michigan State Campus, East Lansing, 48823
Phone (517) 355-5191, ext. 1327
Website www.4hgarden.msu.edu
Hours Daily
Fee Parking, 8 a.m. to 6 p.m.

With more than 60 theme displays, this is a premier children's garden. There are mazes, pots of gold, an alphabet garden, Peter Rabbit garden, and more. With lots of summertime programs, this is a convenient stop for parents with small children.

Anna Scripps Whitcomb Conservatory

Address 876 Picnic Way, Detroit, 48207
Phone (313) 331-7760
Website www.bibsociety.org
Hours Wednesday—Sunday, 10 a.m. to 5 p.m.
Fee No

Built in 1904 and patterned after Thomas Jefferson's greenhouse at Monticello, the Scripps Conservatory sits on Belle Isle, an island park in the Detroit River. It houses one of the United States' orchid collections and has a perennial bed outdoors.

Cooley Gardens

Address 213 W. Main St., Lansing, 48933
Phone (517) 483-4277
Website www.cooleygardens.org
Hours Dawn to dusk ,daily
Fee No

Located just south of Lansing's central business district, Cooley Gardens is an eclectic landscape, typical of formal estate gardens in the early part of the twentieth century. It is composed of garden rooms enclosed by shrubbery, each with a different planting theme.

Cranbrook House and Gardens

Address 380 Lone Pine Rd., Bloomfield Hills, 48304
Phone (248) 645-3147
Website www.cranbrook.edu
Hours Varied
Fee Yes

Cranbrook House and the 40 acres of breathtaking gardens offer a distinctive glimpse into a time when décor and artistry merged. The gardens are filled with colorful, scented blooms, and ornate greenery paired with exquisite fountains and sculpture.

Dahlia Hill

Address 2809 Orchard Dr., Midland, 48640
Phone (989) 631-0100
Website www.dahliahill.org
Hours Dawn to dusk, daily
Fee No

Volunteers planted more than 3,000 dahlias representing at least 250 varieties in eight stone terraces, an iconic image of this garden. Charles Breed's studio and museum are on the grounds along with his sculptures depicting the four seasons.

Dow Gardens

Address 1809 Eastman Ave., Midland, 48640
Phone (800) 362-4874
Website www.dowgardens.org
Hours Tuesday after Labor Day–Oct. 31, 9 a.m. to 4:15 p.m.; Apr. 15–Labor Day, 9 a.m. to 8:30 p.m.
Fee Yes

The Children's Garden was built in 1999 as an organic vegetable garden to teach youngsters where food comes from. More than 200 bedding plants are grown side-by-side in the gardens for evaluations. Perennials, trees, shrubs, and sculpture round out the display.

Edsel and Eleanor Ford Estate

Address 1100 Lake Shore Rd., Grosse Pointe Shores, 48236
Phone (313) 884-4222
Website www.fordhouse.org
Hours Apr.–Dec., Tuesday–Saturday, 9:30 a.m. to 6 p.m., Sunday, 11:30 a.m. to 6 p.m.; Jan.–Mar., Tuesday–Sunday, 11:30 a.m. to 4 p.m.
Fee Yes

Stroll 87 acres of lakefront property to view the design work of famous landscape architect Jens Jensen, architect Albert Kahn, and the art of Cezanne and Diego Rivera. Jensen's garden focuses on the relationship between water and its effects on light and mist.

Grand Hotel

Address 286 Grand Ave., Mackinac Island, 49757
Phone (800) 334-7263
Website www.grandhotel.com
Hours Daily
Fee Yes

The world's largest summer hotel is open from early May to late October. There is a fee for non-guests to visit the 385-room hotel and its iconic, 660-foot-long porch with spectacular views. Lilacs, which bloom in June, are a main attraction in the gardens and on the island.

Hidden Lake Gardens

Address 6214 Monroe Rd. (M-50), Tipton, 49287
Phone (517) 431-2060
Website www.hiddenlakegardens.msu.edu
Hours Apr.–Oct., 8 a.m. to 8:30 p.m.; Nov.–Mar., 8 a.m. to 4 p.m.
Fee Yes, free the first Monday of the month

Hidden Lake is the go-to place to learn about conifers that do well in Midwestern gardens. The collection of large and dwarf types are set in landscape settings. Hosta gardens, bonsai, woods, and wildflowers surround the scenic lake.

Leila Arboretum Society

Address 928 W. Michigan Ave., Battle Creek, 49037
Phone (269) 969-0270
Website www.lasgarden.org
Hours Dawn to dusk, daily
Fee No

Begun in the 1920s by Leila Post, widow of C.W. Post, the founder of the cereal company, the gardens contain annual and perennial borders and a Children's Garden. A labyrinth and the natural history museum Kingman are also on the 72-acre arboretum grounds.

Matthaei Botanical Gardens & Nichols Arboretum

Address 1800 N. Dixboro Rd., Ann Arbor, 48105
Phone (734) 647-7600
Website www.lsa.umich.edu/mbg
Hours Conservatory, Monday, Tuesday, Thursday–Sunday, 10 a.m. to 4:30 p.m., Wednesday, 10 a.m. to 8 p.m.; grounds, sunrise to sunset, daily
Fee Yes, for conservatory; grounds free

The 300-acre Matthaei includes a Knot Garden, prairie demonstration garden, Nichols Arboretum, a gateway garden with North American plants, Rock Garden, Perennial Garden, and Rose Garden. The 123-acre arboretum, bordered by the Huron River, is world-renowned for its collection of peonies.

Michigan State Horticulture Gardens

MICHIGAN

Address Bogue St., Michigan State University, East Lansing, 48823
Phone (517) 355-5191
Website www.hrt.msu.edu/our-gardens
Hours Dawn to dusk, daily
Fee Parking, 8 a.m. to 6 p.m.

The 14 acres of gardens attract thousands of visitors each year and include displays of perennials, annuals, ornamental grasses, Michigan native plants, vegetables, and roses set in numerous theme gardens including the world-famous 4-H Children's Garden voted the most creative ¹/₄ acre garden in Michigan.

Taylor Conservatory and Botanical Gardens

Address 22314 Northline, Taylor, 48180
Phone (888) 383-4108
Website www.taylorconservatory.org
Hours Dawn to dusk, daily
Fee No

More than 1,000 trees and shrubs have been planted at this park in Taylor, including espaliered apple and pear trees. There are more than 100 pots and other seasonal containers planted throughout the gardens, all groomed by volunteers.

Tokushima Saginaw Friendship Garden & Japanese Teahouse

Address 527 Ezra Rust Dr., Saginaw, 48601
Phone (989) 759-1648
Website www.japaneseculturalcenter.org
Hours June–Sept., 9 a.m. to 8 p.m.; Apr., May, Oct. and Nov., Tuesday–Saturday, 9 a.m. to 4 p.m.
Fee Gardens are free

A tea ceremony is presented the second Saturday of each month year-round for a fee, but reservations are required. Nestled on the shore of Lake Linton, this strolling garden has weeping cherry trees, authentic stone lanterns, handcrafted bamboo gates, and an Asian-inspired gazebo.

Veldheer Tulip Center

Address 12755 Quincy St., Holland, 49424
Phone (616) 399-1900
Website www.veldheer.com
Hours May 16–Oct. 15, Monday–Friday, 9 a.m. to 5 p.m.
Fee Yes, for spring bulb display

Late April to mid-May is the best time to visit this center, when 5 *million* tulips, 50,000 daffodils, 10,000 hyacinths and 20,000 crocuses are in full color. The gardens are free in summer and fall, when you can see the buffalo roam. Nearby is DeKlomp, a Delft factory.

Como Park Zoo and Marjorie McNeely Conservatory

Address 1225 Estabrook Dr., St. Paul, 55103
Phone (651) 487-8200
Website www.comozooconservatory.org
Hours Apr.–Sept., 10 a.m. to 6 p.m.;
Oct.–Mar., daily, 10 a.m. to 4 p.m.
Fee Free, donation requested

Como Park Zoo & Conservatory is operated by the Saint Paul Parks and Recreation Department and remains one of the United States' few free metropolitan zoos. The zoo features a seal island, a large cat exhibit, a variety of aquatic life, primates, birds, African hoofed animals, and a world-class polar bear exhibit. The Marjorie McNeely Conservatory is a half-acre indoor and outdoor facility with a number of different wings dedicated to a variety of plant life including bonsai trees, ferns, orchids, and seasonal flowers.

Munsinger Garden & Clemens Garden

Address 1515 Riverside Dr., St. Cloud, 56301
Phone (320) 255-7216
Website www.munsingerclemens.com
Hours Spring–fall, 7 a.m. to 10 p.m.
Fee No

These two gardens are next to each other, offering more than 20 acres of cultivated landscape plantings and natural areas in this Mississippi River town. Munsinger, which dates to the 1930s, has a more naturalistic design. There are 14 acres of flower-bordered paths under pines. Clemens, developed in the 1990s, is more influenced by European design elements. Included are a Rose Garden, White Garden, Formal Garden, Perennial Garden, and Treillage Garden, all with decorative ironwork, sculpture, and fountains.

Eloise Butler Wildflower Garden and Bird Sanctuary

Address 1339 Theodore Wirth Parkway, Minneapolis, 55422
Phone (612) 370-4903
Website www.minneapolisparks.org
Hours Apr. 1–Oct. 15, 7:30 a.m. to an hour before sunset
Fee No

When visitors step behind the rustic gates at Eloise Butler Wildflower Garden and Bird Sanctuary, they quickly forget they're in the middle of the city. The 15-acre garden, with 500 plant species, was founded in 1907 and is the oldest public wildflower garden in the nation.

Linnaeus Arboretum

Address 800 W. College Ave., St. Peter, 56082
Phone (507) 933-6181
Website www.gustavus.edu/arboretum
Hours Daylight hours, daily
Fee No

The arboretum at Gustavus Adolphus College is named for Linnaeus, the Swedish botanist who devised the system by which plants are named. The natural ecosystems represented include conifer forests, prairies, and deciduous forests. Formal gardens surround the Melva Lind Interpretive Center.

Living Legacy Gardens

Address 1830 Airport Rd., Staples, 56479
Phone (218) 894-5161 or (800) 247-6836, ext. 5161
Website www.clcmn.edu/busind/livinglegacy.html
Hours Daylight
Fee No

Located at the Central Lakes College Agricultural Center, two miles north of Staples, the gardens demonstrate perennials, annuals, herbs, shrubs, vines, fruits, native plants, and trees hardy to USDA Zone 3, as well as various landscaping styles.

Minnesota Landscape Arboretum

Address 3675 Arboretum Dr., Chaska, 55318
Phone (952) 443-1400
Website www.arboretum.umn.edu
Hours 8 a.m. to 8 p.m. or sunset, whichever is earlier
Fee Yes

Tour 1,000 acres of gardens, model landscapes, woodlands, wetlands, prairie, and extensive collections of northern-hardy plants. Sculpture and other art are placed throughout the arboretum. Free admission after 4:30 p.m. on several Thursdays during the summer, and all Thursdays from November through March. You can tour the arboretum via its $12^{1}/_{2}$ miles of trails.

Crosby Arboretum

Address 370 Ridge Rd., Picayune, 39466
Phone (601) 799-2311
Website www.crosbyarboretum.msstate.edu
Hours Wednesday–Sunday, 9 a.m. to 5 p.m. or by reservation
Fee No

The Crosby Arboretum preserves, protects, and displays plants native to the Pearl River Drainage Basin ecosystem. The arboretum includes savanna, woodland, and aquatic exhibits. Longleaf pine forests, slash pine hardwoods, sweetbay, tupelo, swampbay, beech-magnolia, bald cypress-tupelo, bottomland hardwoods, hillside bogs, and savannas are just some of the forest types represented. Drastic and subtle changes in landscape patterns can be observed within each exhibit. In addition to the 104-acre interpretive site, the Arboretum also collectively maintains 700 acres of off-site natural areas that are preserved for scientific study.

MISSISSIPPI

Mynelle Gardens

Address 4736 Clinton Blvd., Jackson, 39209
Phone (601) 960-1894
Website www.city.jackson.ms.us/visitors/mynellgardens
Hours Mar.–Oct., Monday–Saturday, 9 a.m. to 5 p.m.,
Sunday, noon to 5 p.m.; Nov.–Feb., Monday–Saturday,
8 a.m. to 4 p.m., Sunday, noon to 4 p.m.; Dec.–Feb., closed Sunday
Fee Yes

This 7-acre collage of several distinct botanical gardens includes winding pathways, cascading pools, and distinctive bridges that lead across the pond to an island oasis. It typifies the southern garden with features worth emulating. Mynelle Gardens is a wildlife sanctuary and a haven for songbirds. In years past, the Westbrook House, built in 1917, was the scene of garden parties, civic fundraisers, and therapy for World War II recovering soldiers.

Missouri Botanical Garden

MISSOURI

Address 4344 Shaw Blvd., St. Louis, 63110
Phone (314) 577-5100 or (800) 642-8842
Website www.mobot.org
Hours 9 a.m. to 5 p.m. daily
Fee Yes

Considered one of the premier botanical gardens in the United States, the Missouri Botanical Garden was founded in 1859 as a public garden for enjoyment and as a place to study plants. The 1/2-acre Climatron, a geodesic dome inspired by Buckminster Fuller, holds 1,400 plant species as well as birds and other animals. Tower Grove House and its Victorian District Garden reflect the nineteenth century. The Children's Garden blends nineteenth-century history and botany as well as a venture into a limestone cave.

Botanical Gardens at Nathanael Greene Close Memorial Park

Address 2400 S. Scenic Ave., Springfield, 65807
 Phone (417) 891-1515
Website www.friendsofthegarden.org
  Hours Monday–Saturday, 8 a.m. to 8 p.m., Sunday, 11 a.m. to 6 p.m.
   Fee Park is free, fee for gardens

This 114-acre site includes Master Gardener Demonstration Gardens, Mizumoto Japanese Stroll Garden, Dr. Bill Roston Native Butterfly House, Gray-Campbell Farmstead, and dozens of specialty gardens. NatureGround is a combination of education and play for children.

Ewing and Muriel Kauffman Memorial Garden

Address 4801 Rockhill Rd., Kansas City, 64110
 Phone (816) 932-1000
Website www.kauffman.org/about-foundation/kauffman-legacy-park.aspx
  Hours 8 a.m. to dusk
   Fee No

The Ewing and Muriel Kauffman Memorial Garden is an exquisite area of Kauffman Legacy Park. It features bronze sculptures by Tom Corbin among lush and colorful annual and perennial plantings, pruned foliage framed by stone walls, and playful fountains. In all, there are about 7,000 plants of more than 300 varieties, including heirlooms.

Mizzou Botanic Garden

Address Reynolds Alumni Center, University of Missouri, Columbia, 65201
Phone (573) 882-4240
Website www.gardens.missouri.edu
Hours Year-round
Fee No

There are 11 thematic and 7 special collection gardens throughout the Mizzou campus. Points of special interest include the Beetle Bailey Garden, with a sculpture of the famed cartoon character sitting at a table, Wildlife Pond, Jesse Hall Container Garden, Asiatic and Oriental Lily Garden, and the Hardy Geranium Collection. There are several state champion trees on campus. (Pick up a map of the gardens at the Alumni Center.)

Powell Gardens

Address 1609 N.W. U.S. 50, Kingsville, 64061
Phone (816) 697-2600
Website www.powellgardens.org
Hours May–Sept., daily, 9 a.m. to 6 p.m.; Oct.–Apr., 9 a.m. to 5 p.m.
Fee Yes

The Heartland Harvest Garden features a Quilt Garden and an Author's Garden, where writers design a plot based on their philosophy. Elsewhere, explore the interactive Fountain Garden or trek a 3¼-mile nature trail that has prairie pockets, lotus- and frog-filled ponds, an Osage orange woodland, and meadows.

MONTANA

Tizer Botanic Gardens & Arboretum

Address 38 Tizer Rd., Jefferson City, 59638
Phone (406) 933-8789 or (866) 933-8789
Website www.tizergardens.com
Hours Mother's Day–end of Sept., 10 a.m. to 6 p.m., daily
Fee Yes

More than 14 gardens make up this botanical jewel in the Elkhorn Mountains along Prickly Pear Creek. The garden participates in the Plant Select program of the Denver Botanic Garden by evaluating Montana-worthy garden plants. You'll enjoy the vegetable, herb, rose, and meditation gardens. Hummingbirds and butterflies frequent the hummingbird garden.

Daly Mansion

Address 251 Eastside Hwy., Hamilton, 59840, 59840
Phone (406) 363-6004
Website www.dalymansion.org
Hours May–Oct., 10 a.m. to 3 p.m., daily
Fee Yes

Located on 46 acres of lush landscape, the Daly Mansion is the historic home of nineteenth-century American industrialist Marcus Daly. The exhibits here convey how he lived in his house and gardens.

Memorial Rose Garden

Address 700 Brook St., Missoula, 59807
Phone (406) 552-6000
Website www.ci.missoula.mt.us/index.aspx?NID=181
Hours Daylight
Fee No

Memorial Rose Garden Park was established in 1944 by the city and the Missoula Rose Society to commemorate members of the armed forces killed in World War II. Since then, it has become the site for memorials dedicated to casualties of Vietnam, Grenada, Panama, the Persian Gulf, and Korea. More than 2,000 roses in several beds are maintained by the Missoula Rose Society.

Lauritzen Gardens

Address 100 Bancroft St., Omaha, 68108

Phone (402) 346-4002

Website www.lauritzengardens.org

Hours Daily, 9 a.m. to 5 p.m.; mid-May–mid-Sept., Mondays and Tuesday, until 8 p.m.

Fee Yes

Lauritzen Gardens celebrates history with a Lewis and Clark icon, one of nine on the Lewis and Clark Interpretive Trail along the Missouri River. Visitors can create their own journey of discovery along the trail while learning about the historic expedition. Other points of interest are several sculptures placed throughout the garden, an English perennial border, and the Children's Garden with "Dina," a dinosaur made from scrap metal and farm pieces. Seven trains run through the Model Railroad Garden during the summer.

Arbor Day Farm

Address 2611 Arbor Ave., Nebraska City, 68410
Phone (402) 873-8757
Website www.arbordayfarm.org
Hours Monday–Saturday, 9 a.m. to 5 p.m., Sunday, 11 a.m. to 5 p.m.
Fee Yes

Where else can you climb a treehouse 50 feet high? Also fun is "Trees in the Movies," where 90 scenes from 66 classic movies in which trees are center stage are screened. The one-hour Discovery Ride takes visitors through the 260-acre Arbor Day Farm. There are miles of scenic nature trails.

Joslyn Castle

Address 3902 Davenport St., Omaha, 68131
Phone (402) 595-2199
Website www.joslyncastle.com
Hours First and third Sundays of the month for tours, 1 p.m., 2 p.m., and 3 p.m.
Fee Yes

Lynhurst is the official name of this 35-room 1903 Scottish-style home that locals call Joslyn. Well-known landscape architect Jens Jensen designed the 5½-acre landscape. However, a storm in 2008 destroyed many of the mature trees, and a renovation is underway.

Gardens at the Springs Preserve

Address 333 S. Valley View Blvd. at US 90, Las Vegas, 89152
Phone (702) 822-7700
Website www.springspreserve.org
Hours 10 a.m. to 6 p.m. daily
Fee Yes

Gardens for cactus, palms, herbs, roses, food, an enabling garden, and various types of landscapes make up the 8-acre Gardens at the Springs Preserve, a compound that also has a theatre, museums, and a desert living center. There's a celebration of plants from the Mojave and an emphasis on water conservation. The Origen Museum Living Collections includes native mammals, reptiles, and invertebrates such as a Lizard Habitat, Desert Cottontail, Gray Fox, Pocket Gopher, Ant Colony, Gila Monsters, and Night Life wildlife.

Ethel M® Botanical Cactus Garden

Address 2 Cactus Dr., Henderson, 89014
  Phone (702) 435-2655
Website www.ethelm.com/about_us/cactus_garden.aspx
  Hours 8:30 a.m. to 6 p.m. daily
    Fee No

This is probably the only cactus garden built around a chocolate factory, but that's exactly what visitors will find. The 4-acre garden has what's called a "living machine," a bio-based wastewater treatment method to recycle its wastewater. More than 300 species are represented.

University of Nevada Las Vegas Arboretum

Address 4505 S. Maryland Pkwy., Las Vegas, 89154
  Phone (702) 895-3392
Website www.facilities.unlv.edu/landscape/arboretum
  Hours Daily
    Fee No

A highlight of the arboretum is the Xeric Garden, specially designed with drought-tolerant plants, efficient irrigation, and other methods to conserve water while still promoting a beautiful landscape. The garden is located near the Barrick Museum of Natural History and the Harry Reid Center for Environmental Studies.

The Fells

Address 456 Route 103A, Newbury, 03255
Phone (603) 763-4789
Website www.thefells.org
Hours Gardens and trails, 9 a.m. to 5 p.m. daily
Fee Yes

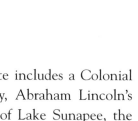

This fine example of an American Country Estate includes a Colonial Revival home and gardens of John Milton Hay, Abraham Lincoln's secretary of state. Resting on the eastern shore of Lake Sunapee, the varied and wonderful gardens include a field of heather, rose terrace, rock garden, old garden, and a 100-foot-long perennial border. Across the way is a 1$\frac{1}{2}$-mile trail through the John Hay National Wildlife Refuge and two 300- to 400-year-old hemlocks.

Saint-Gaudens National Historic Site

Address 139 Saint-Gaudens Rd., Cornish, 03745
Phone (603) 675-2175
Website www.sgnns.org
Hours Memorial Day–Oct. 31, 9 a.m. to 4:30 p.m. daily;
gardens until dusk
Fee Yes

This is the home of Augustus Saint-Gaudens, a noted artist most famous for the Standing Lincoln sculpture and other heroic-sized monuments. He's also known as the designer of the 1907 U.S. $20 gold piece, deemed the most beautiful coin ever. More than 100 works of the sculptor are exhibited in the galleries and on the grounds at Saint-Gaudens. There are two hiking trails through wildlife-filled fields and wetlands. The gardens and lawns showcase hundreds of species.

Fuller Gardens

Address 10 Willow Ave., North Hampton, 03862
   Phone (603) 964-5414
Website www.fullergardens.org
   Hours Mid-May to mid-Oct., 10 a.m. to 5:30 p.m. daily
      Fee Yes

This early-twentieth-century Colonial Revival estate includes seaside gardens designed by landscape architect Arthur Shurcliff and, in the 1930s, the Olmsted Brothers firm. Sculpted hedges help define gardens for roses, perennials, annuals and hostas. There's also a Japanese garden and conservatory.

Moffatt-Ladd House & Garden

Address 154 Market St., Portsmouth, 03801
   Phone (603) 436-8221
Website www.moffattladd.org
   Hours Mid-June–mid-Oct., Monday–Saturday, 11 a.m. to 5 p.m., Sunday, 1 p.m. to 5 p.m.
      Fee Yes

Old English damask roses planted in 1768 and a horse chestnut tree planted in 1776 remain on this nineteenth-century estate. Initially the garden had passalong plants from original owner Alexander Hamilton Ladd's mother and grandmother. The three-story Georgian mansion has many original family furnishings and rare hall and chamber wallpapers.

Prescott Park

Address 105 Marcy St., Portsmouth, 03801
Phone (603) 431-8748
Website www.prescottparknh.org
Hours Daily
Fee No

The Prescott sisters purchased and cleared land along the Piscataqua River to form a public waterfront and park, free and accessible. In the center of the park are the formal gardens, pathways, and fountains. The 10-acre Prescott Park is also home to an extensive summer arts festival.

Strawbery Banke Museum

Address 14 Hancock St., Portsmouth, 03801
Phone (603) 433-1100
Website www.strawberybanke.org
Hours May 1–Oct. 31, 10 a.m. to 5 p.m. daily
Fee Yes

Rescued from an ill-fated urban renewal project, Strawbery Banke demonstrates a typical American neighborhood throughout four centuries. Through restored houses, exhibits, historic landscapes, and gardens, it tells the stories of the many generations who settled in Portsmouth from the late seventeenth to the mid-twentieth century. A Victory garden recreates the World War II effort using period-appropriate plants.

Garden for the Blind and Physically Handicapped

Address 1081 Green St., Iselin, 08830

Phone (732) 283-1796

Website www.woodbridgegardenclub.org

Hours Year-round, daily

Fee No

The Woodbridge Garden Club maintains the garden, which is adjacent to the Iselin Branch Library. The garden is certified as a Monarch Way Station and a Wildlife Habitat. The Sensory Garden has descriptive identifications in Braille. It includes rose, perennial, and cottage gardens.

Grounds For Sculpture

Address 18 Fairgrounds Rd., Hamilton, 08619
Phone (609) 586-0616
Website www.groundsforsculpture.org
Hours Year-round, Tuesday–Sunday, 10 a.m. to 6 pm.
Fee Yes

Founder J. Seward Johnson developed the 35-acre garden to showcase contemporary sculpture. Since it opened in 1992 at the former New Jersey State Fairgrounds, the park has built a collection of over 240 works, including George Segal and other renowned artists. Some of the works in the collection were commissioned specifically for the sculpture park. Careful attention has been paid to trees and shrubs so that the plants enhance the art. There are also indoor seasonal displays and special tours for children and the blind.

Leaming's Run Gardens

Address 1845 Route 9, North Cape May Court House, 08210
 Phone (609) 465-5871
Website www.leamingsrungardens.com
  Hours Mid-May–mid-Oct., 9:30 a.m. to 7 p.m. daily
     Fee Yes

Reputed to have the largest public annual garden in the United States, Leaming's Run serves as an outdoor classroom where families can learn about plants and wildlife. It features 25 themed gardens, a fernery, and a shady bamboo grove. Take a trip back to the eighteenth century at Colonial Farm, where you'll find historically correct crops and animals. During August, ruby-throated hummingbirds come to feed before they migrate south on their annual journey. They sometimes stay through mid-September.

Presby Memorial Iris Gardens

Address 474 Upper Mountain Ave., Upper Montclair, 07043
Phone (973) 783-5974
Website www.presbyirisgardens.org
Hours Year-round
Fee No

Inspired by horticulturist Frank H. Presby, a volunteer citizens group started the garden in 1927. Today, there are 10,000 irises, representing about 3,000 varieties that produce more than 100,000 flowers throughout the season. Presby was a founder of the American Iris Society. In his honor, volunteers planted bearded, Siberian, Louisiana, and Japanese irises, each of which has a different bloom time to extend the season well into summer. The living museum is on the National Register of Historic Places. Iris rhizomes are periodically for sale as they are dug from Presby's beds.

Rutgers Gardens

Address 112 Ryders Lane, New Brunswick, 08901
Phone (732) 932-8451
Website www.rutgersgardens.rutgers.edu
Hours Year-round, 8:30 a.m. to dusk
Fee No

Visitors will find the world's largest collection of American hollies along with azaleas, rhododendrons, oaks, beeches, conifers, lindens, and a Chinese toon ("tree vegetable"). The collection of ornamental trees—those that are usually shorter than 30 feet tall—is helpful for homeowners with smaller landscapes, and desirable for smaller landscapes. The Ella Quimby Water Conservation Terrace Gardens features drought-tolerant plants. There's also a Rain Garden and Bamboo Forest. The Donald B. Lacey Display Garden boasts the largest planting of annuals in the country.

Van Vleck House & Gardens

Address 21 Van Vleck St., Montclair, 07042
Phone (973) 744-4752
Website www.vanvleck.org
Hours Year-round, dawn to dusk
Fee No

The property was developed 140 years ago, but the only building that remains is the U-shaped Italiante villa. Now a 6-acre site, many of the historic gardens have been restored and maintained by the Montclair Foundation. These include the Courtyard Garden, Formal Garden, Azalea Walk, Carriage House and Greenhouses, Woodlands Garden, Mother's Garden and Upper Lawn, Drying Yard, Butterfly Garden, and Flower and Water Garden. Howard Van Vleck hybridized several rhododendrons, some of which survive in the gardens.

Camden Children's Garden

Address 3 Riverside Dr., Camden, 08103
Phone (865) 365-8733
Website www.camdenchildrensgarden.org
Hours Friday–Sunday, 10 a.m. to 4 p.m., Thursdays by reservation
Fee Yes

The Camden City Garden Club operates the Children's Garden, which has a special emphasis on education activities that relate to nature. Benjamin Franklin's Secret Garden and Workshop is in the waterfront garden along with the Philadelphia Eagles Four Seasons Butterfly House.

Colonial Park Arboretum and Gardens

Address 150 Mettiers Rd., Somerset, 08873
Phone (732) 873-2459
Website www.somersetcountyparks.org/parksFacilities/colonial/ColonialPark.html
Hours Sunrise to sunset, daily
Fee No

This 685-acre park includes scenic frontage of the historic Delaware and Raritan Canal and the Millstone River. Prize-winning horticultural displays and pristine natural areas are spaced amid the broad lawns and ponds of this diverse Somerset County park. There are a variety of plant collections.

Cross Estate Gardens

Address Old Jockey Hollow Rd., Bernardsville, 07924
Phone (973) 376-0308
Website www.crossestategardens.org
Hours Dawn to dusk, daily
Fee No

This early-twentieth-century landscape of the Cross Estate, characteristic of the Arts and Crafts period, includes a formal perennial garden, a wisteria-covered pergola, a mountain laurel allée, hiking trails, and a garden of native plants. A self-guided walk showcases historic trees.

Frelinghuysen Arboretum

Address 353 E. Hanover Ave., Morris Township, 07962
Phone (973) 326-7601
Website www.arboretumfriends.org
Hours Gardens 9 a.m. to dusk
Fee No

 The beautiful 127-acre Frelinghuysen Arboretum offers visitors a serene place to relax as well as learn more about plants well suited to the soils and climate of the area. Surrounding a magnificent Colonial Revival mansion are woodlands, meadows, gardens, and distinctive collections of trees and shrubs.

Greenwood Gardens

Address 274 Old Short Hills Rd., Short Hills, 07078
Phone (973) 258-4026
Website www.greenwoodgardens.org
Hours May–Oct. by reservation only
Fee Yes

There is a major capital campaign underway to restore the gardens and stabilize structures, including the Arts and Crafts–era home. Visitors stroll formal gardens and gaze over wide, stepped terraces, moss-covered reflecting pools, and perennial beds to the wooded hillsides of the Watchung Mountains.

James Rose Center

Address 506 E. Ridgewood Ave., Ridgewood, 07450
Phone (201) 446-6017
Website www.jamesrosecenter.org
Hours Mid-May–late Oct., Tuesday–Sunday, 10 a.m. to 4 p.m.
Fee Yes

The design and landscape research center was founded by James Rose, a prominent twentieth-century landscape architect. He is credited with promoting and incorporating modern expressionism as an alternative approach to post-war suburban residential development. The designs of this early pioneer of landscape architecture still feel radical.

Laurelwood Arboretum

Address 725 Pines Lake Dr. West, Wayne, 07470
Phone (973) 202-9579
Website www.laurelwoodarboretum.org
Hours Dawn to dusk, daily
Fee No

This 30-acre arboretum features woodland trails and gardens, wildlife, two ponds, streams, and hundreds of varieties of rhododendrons, azaleas, and other unusual species of plants and trees. Gravel paths wind and connect through the Arboretum, making it an ideal destination for hikers, runners, birdwatchers, plant enthusiasts, and photographers.

Leonard Buck Garden

Address 11 Layton Rd., Far Hills, 07931
Phone (908) 234-2677
Website www.somersetcountyparks.org/parksfacilities/buck/LJBuck.html
Hours Monday–Friday. 10 a.m. to 4 p.m., Saturday, 10 a.m. to 5 p.m., Sunday, noon to 5 p.m.; Dec.–Mar., closed weekends
Fee No

The Leonard J. Buck Garden is one of the premier rock gardens in the eastern United States. Begun in the late 1930s, the garden has reached a breathtaking point of maturity. It consists of a series of alpine and woodland gardens situated in a 33-acre wooded stream valley.

NEW JERSEY

Macculloch Hall Historical Museum and Gardens

Address 45 Macculloch Ave., Morristown, 07960
Phone (973) 538-2404
Website www.macullochhall.org
Hours Wednesday, Thursday, and Sunday, 1 p.m. to 4 p.m.
Fee Yes; gardens free

Three acres of colorful and elegant gardens remain of the estate, including several heirloom roses that date before the 1920s. Inside, visitors will find the largest collection of Thomas Nast cartoons. The museum founder also collected fine porcelain, rugs, and historical presidential documents.

New Jersey Botanical Garden

Address 2 Morris Rd., Ringwood, 07456
Phone (973) 962-9534
Website www.njbg.org
Hours 8 a.m. to 8 p.m. daily
Fee Free, but fee for parking on weekends and holidays; fee for house tour

Skyland estate contains 13 gardens, including a carefully restored rock garden, which surrounds an Octagonal Pool and was designed so that small plants would be waist high. The Winter Garden is a collection of forms, textures, and colors to stimulate the senses in winter.

Prospect House & Garden

Address Princeton University, Washington St., Princeton, 08544
Phone (609) 258-3455
Website www.princeton.edu/prospect house
Hours Gardens, Year-round
Fee Free for gardens

The former home of the presidents of Princeton University is a restaurant, but the gardens remain and are open to the public. Ellen Wilson, wife of former Princeton president Woodrow Wilson, laid out the flower garden. She also created a garden in the shape of the university seal. Yearly, 8,000 flowers are planted.

Reeves-Reed Arboretum

Address 165 Hobart Ave., Summit, 07901
Phone (908) 273-8787
Website www.reeves-reedarboretum.org
Hours Dawn to dusk, daily
Fee No

The century-old Wisner House, Keller Azalea Garden, and the Reeves-Reed Rock Garden have been restored recently. Reeves-Reed Arboretum has 5^1/$_2$-acres of formal gardens representing design trends of the time. (Gates at entrance are to keep deer out. Step to the painted white line and the gates will open.)

Sister Mary Grace Burns Arboretum

Address 900 Lakewood Ave., Lakewood, 08701
Phone (800) 458-8422
Website www.georgian.edu/arboretum
Hours Year-round, 8 a.m. to dusk
Fee No

Georgian Court was the winter home of millionaire George Jay Gould. After his death, it was purchased by the Sisters of Mercy of New Jersey and converted to a college. Plants, statues, fountains, and bridges adorn the estate, but there is also a good collection of native plants of the Pine Barrens.

Well-Sweep Herb Farm

Address 205 Mount Bethel Rd., Port Murray, 07865
Phone (908) 852-5390
Website www.wellsweep.com/
Hours Year-round, Monday–Saturday, 9 a.m. to 5 p.m.; Jan.–Mar., please call first
Fee Free

With more than 1,949 varieties, Well-Sweep boasts one of the largest collections of herbs and perennials in the United States. Founded in 1969, visitors can see butterfly, medicinal, and knot gardens, as well as more than 70 scented geraniums on the family-owned farm.

Wick House Herb Garden

Address Tempe Wick Rd., Morristown, 07960
Phone (973) 543-4030
Website www.nps.gov/morr/index.htm
Hours 9 a.m. to 5 p.m. daily
Fee No

The Morristown National Historical Park maintains the Wick House Herb Garden, an eighteenth-century planting of herbs and vegetables. Morristown's Jockey Hollow area includes a wealth of history, nature, and recreation, including a colonial life experience at the soldiers huts.

Willowwood Arboretum

Address 300 Longview Rd., Chester, 07930
Phone (908) 234-0992
Website www.morrisparks.net/aspparks/wwmain.asp
Hours Dawn to dusk, daily; Conservatory, 9 a.m. to 4 p.m., weekdays
Fee No

With 130 acres, Willowwood has about 3,500 types of native and exotic plants. There's a swath of undisturbed forest and collections of oak, maples, firs, pines, willows, magnolias, ferns, wildflowers, and a 98-foot-tall dawn redwood.

Rio Grande Botanic Garden

Address ABQ Park, 2601 Central Ave., NW, Albuquerque, 87104
Phone (505) 764-6200
Website www.cabq.gov/biopark/garden
Hours 9 a.m. to 5 p.m. daily; Memorial Day–Labor Day,
Saturday and Sunday until 6 p.m.
Fee Yes

The 36-acre garden has 10 areas, including Mediterranean and Desert conservatories. The Rio Grande Heritage Farm takes visitors to the 1930s, and a 14-foot-tall topiary dragon stands at Children's Fantasy Garden. The Old World Walled Garden offers a cool retreat with a Spanish-Moorish style. Curandera Garden demonstrates Spanish folk medicine and includes a bas-relief sculpture by Diego Rivera. The 4-acre Sasebo Japanese Garden offers a meditative respite. The Botanic Garden is in BioPark, which also has a beach, aquarium, and zoo.

Santa Fe Botanical Garden/
Leonora Curtin Wetland Preserve

Address 27283 I-25 West Frontage Rd., Santa Fe, 87507
Phone (505) 471-9103
Website www.santafebotanicalgarden.org
Hours May 1–Oct. 31, Saturday, 9 a.m. to noon,
Sunday, 1 p.m. to 4 p.m.
Fee No

This 35-acre preserve south of Santa Fe contains three types of plant communities: riparian-wetland, transitional, and dry uplands. It's near a rare, nature marsh that adds to the diversity of plants and wildlife. Only docent-led tours are allowed at Ortiz Mountains Education Preserve 30 miles southwest of Santa Fe, where black bear, coyote, horned toads, and antlions roam. In late 2011, the Santa Fe Botanical Garden will break ground at Museum Hill on a new 12-acre site.

Albuquerque Rose Garden

Address 8205 Apache Ave., NE, Albuquerque, 87110
Phone (505) 255-9233
Website www.albuquerquerose.com
Hours Daily
Fee No

Located at the Tony Hillerman Library, the garden opened in 1995 in advance of the American Rose Society National Convention. Raised planters allow for good viewing of miniature and polyantha roses and a 10-foot pergola showcases climbing roses. Fragrant Way has exceptional hybrid teas.

Salman's Santa Fe Greenhouses

Address 2904 Rufina St., Santa Fe, 87104
Phone (877) 811-2700; (505) 473-2700
Website www.santafegreenhouses.com
Hours Monday–Saturday 8 a.m. to 5:30 p.m., Sunday, 10 a.m. to 5 p.m.
Fee No

The Inspiration Garden includes dozens of retailer High Country Gardens' plants, which were developed onsite or introduced by owner David Salman. The Xeric Demonstration Garden includes the Cold-Hardy Mediterranean Garden, which recently won the MGA Green Thumb Award.

Brooklyn Botanic Garden

Address 900 Washington Ave., Brooklyn, 11225
Phone (718) 623-7200
Website www.bbg.org
Hours Tuesday–Friday, 8 a.m. to 6 p.m., Saturday–Sunday, 10 a.m. to 6 p.m.
Fee Yes

The 52-acre Brooklyn Botanic Garden celebrated its 100th birthday in 2010 and has undertaken several renovation projects to ensure its next 100 years. A relocated and redesigned Herb Garden reflects the world cultures of Brooklyn neighborhoods. The Cranford Rose Garden has also been renovated. A dozen garden areas are on the grounds along with the conservatory, which holds an aquatic house, bonsai, tropical plants, and more. Collections include magnolias, orchids, roses, lilacs, tree peonies, and flowering cherries.

Buffalo and Erie County Botanical Gardens

Address 2655 S. Park Ave., Buffalo, 14218
Phone (716) 827-1584, ext. 206
Website www.buffalogardens.com
Hours Monday–Sunday, 10 a.m. to 5 p.m.
Fee Yes

The most spectacular aspect of this garden is the tri-domed conservatory, one of only two remaining in the United States. In the nine greenhouses, visitors will see collections of palms, Florida Everglades, Panama Cloud Forest and Epiphytes, orchids, begonias, ferns, and desert plants. The conservatory also holds the world's largest collection of ivies, with 400 varieties on display. Outdoors is a rose garden, perennial and shrub border, arboretum, and children's garden. Frederick Law Olmsted designed the public park system in Buffalo.

Central Park Conservatory Garden

Address 5th Ave. and 105th St., NYC, 10029

Phone (212) 310-6600

Website www.centralparknyc.org/visit/things-to-see/north-end/
conservatory-garden.html

Hours 6 a.m. to 1 a.m. daily

Fee No

This 1898 garden reflects three distinct landscaping styles: Italian, English, and French. The Italian garden has a wisteria pergola, lawn bordered by clipped yew hedges, two allées of pink and white crabapples, and a 12-foot-high jet fountain. The focal point of the English garden is the Burnett Fountain, a sculpture of a boy playing a pipe to attract birds and a girl offering a bowl of water for them to drink. The French garden is a spectacular show of tulips in spring and mums in fall.

Cloisters Museum & Gardens

Address 99 Margaret Corbin Dr., Fort Tryon Park, NYC, 10040
Phone (212) 923-3700; TTY (212) 570-3828
Website www.metmuseum.org/cloisters
Hours Mar.–Oct., Tuesday–Sunday, 9:30 a.m. to 5:15 p.m.;
Nov.–Feb., Tuesday–Sunday, 9:30 a.m. to 4:45 p.m.
Fee Yes

A visit to the Cloisters is like a trip to medieval Europe. This branch of the Metropolitan Museum of Art has collected art and architecture from the twelfth to the fifteenth centuries, including many religious pieces. The gardens, which are enclosed or cloistered, take their cues from elements in the collection's medieval art. For instance, English daisies are seen in many pieces of art, and these have been planted in one of the gardens.

Mohonk Preserve

Address 3197 Rt. 44/55, Mohonk Visitor Center, Gardiner, 12525
Phone (845) 255-0919
Website www.mohonkpreserve.org
Hours Sunrise to sunset, daily
Fee Yes

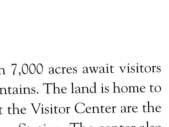

Stunning views, relaxation, and adventure on 7,000 acres await visitors to Mohonk Preserve in the Shawangunk Mountains. The land is home to more than 1,400 plant and animal species. At the Visitor Center are the Kid's Discovery Corner and a Weather Learning Station. The center also is home to a sensory trail, butterfly garden, and nature trail. The preserve specializes in hikes, bicycle rides, and rock climbing. Adjacent is the resort hotel, Mohonk Mountain Home, which has day passes for its gardens.

New York Botanical Garden

Address 2900 Southern Blvd., Bronx, 10458
Phone (718) 817-8700
Website www.nybg.org
Hours Tuesday–Sunday, 10 a.m. to 6 p.m.
Fee Yes

Founded in 1891, the NYBG is the largest of any botanical garden in any city in the United States. It has 50 gardens and collections containing more than 1 million plants. Special displays include the conifer arboretum, rock garden, rose garden, and a border garden. The conservatory, which opened in 1902 and was restored in 1997, is one of only two remaining tri-dome Victorian glass structures. Another facility, the Nolen Greenhouses for Living Collectibles, which opened in 2005, holds more than 8,000 orchids.

Noguchi Museum and Sculpture Garden

Address 9-01 33rd Rd., Long Island City, 11106
Phone (718) 204-7088
Website www.noguchi.org
Hours Wednesday–Friday, 10 a.m. to 5 p.m.,
Saturday and Sunday, 11 a.m. to 6 p.m.
Fee Yes

A converted, 27,000-square-foot, two-story industrial building in Queens is home to 10 galleries and a celebrated, open-air sculpture garden designed by the famous Japanese-American artist Isamu Noguchi. The galleries contain Noguchi's sculptures, architectural models, stage designs, drawings, furniture, and lamps. Visitors enter through the sculpture garden and view Noguchi-selected pieces of art. Other galleries have regular exhibitions of contemporary artists. In 2008, the garden lost its 75-year-old tree of heaven, but the wood was used to create benches throughout the museum and grounds.

Planting Fields Arboretum

Address 1395 Planting Fields Rd., Oyster Bay, 11771
Phone (516) 922-8600
Website www.plantingfields.org
Hours 9 a.m. to 5 p.m. daily
Fee Yes, for parking

Coe Hall and the Planting Fields gardens comprise one of the few remaining estates along the Gold Coast of Long Island's North Shore. The 409 acres are intact. The Tudor Revival mansion with a mostly Elizabethan interior has many original murals, stone carvings, and ironwork. The stained glass windows date from the thirteenth to the nineteenth centuries. The grounds have rolling lawns, formal gardens, and hiking trails. Seasonal displays are the highlights of the camellia and main greenhouses.

Queens Botanical Garden

Address 43-50 Main St., Flushing, 11355

Phone (718) 886-3800

Website www.queensbotanical.org

Hours Apr. 1–Oct. 31, Tuesday– Sunday, 8 a.m. to 6 p.m.;
Nov. 1–Mar. 31, Tuesday–Sunday, 8 a.m. to 4:30 p.m.

Fee Yes

The 39-acre Queens Botanical Garden, created as part of the 1939 World's Fair, contains two dozen themed areas, including a Children's Garden, Fragrance Walk, Bioswales, Backyard Gardens, All-America Selections Trial Garden, Compost Demonstration Gardens, Senior Garden, and the Green Roof Plant Collection. Many of the planting designs are original to 1939. With an emphasis on sustainable living and landscaping, the garden opened a new Visitor Center in 2007, the first Platinum LEED building in New York City.

Vanderbilt Mansion Gardens

Address Rt. 9, Hyde Park, 12538
Phone (845) 229-7770
Website www.nps.gov/vama/index.htm
Hours Grounds, daily, sunrise to sunset; mansion, daily,
9 a.m. to 5 p.m.; tours limited Nov.–Mar.
Fee Yes

This National Park Service site overlooks the Hudson River and the Catskill Mountains and is a wonderful example of the Gilded Age that followed the industrialization of the United States. The Frederick W. Vanderbilt Garden Association at Marist College was formed to restore the gardens. Volunteers plant annual display gardens each year, and they have restored many of the historic gardens, including the Italian Garden, perennial garden, and the two-tiered Rose Garden. The mansion reflects Beaux-Arts architecture.

Wave Hill

Address W. 249th St. and Independence Ave., Bronx, 10470

Phone (718) 549-3200

Website www.wavehill.org

Hours Mid-Apr.–mid-Oct., Tuesday–Sunday, 9 a.m. to 5:30 p.m.; mid-Oct.–mid-Apr., 9 a.m. to 4 p.m.

Fee Yes

Overlooking the Hudson River and the New Jersey Palisades sits the 28-acre Wave Hill, a turn-of-the-twentieth-century estate and garden, which are designed for an intimacy of scale. Highlights include flower gardens, forests, a 10-acre woodland, aquatic and monocot specimens, and pergola-framed vistas. The Marco Polo Stufano Conservatory shelters tender plants from around the world. A wild garden allows a light hand for tending the self-sowing annuals and perennials, including many native plants. The hillside garden and gazebo in this area have been there since 1915.

Binghamton Zoo at Ross Park

Address 185 Park Ave., Binghamton, 13903
Phone (607) 724-5454
Website www.rossparkzoo.com
Hours 10 a.m. to 5 p.m. daily
Fee Yes

This is the fifth-oldest zoo in the United States, but like a lot of zoos these days, it has as many interesting gardens as it does animals. Hosta, iris, ornamental grass, and a butterfly garden are on the grounds.

Boscobel House and Gardens

Address 1601 Rt. 9D, Garrison, 10524
Phone (845) 265-3638
Website www.boscobel.org
Hours Apr.–Oct., 9:30 a.m. to 5 p.m.; Nov.–Dec., 9:30 a.m. to 4 p.m.; Jan.–Mar., closed
Fee Yes

The 1804 Federalist/Neo-Classical house was dismantled, moved from Montrose to Garrison, rebuilt, and a new landscape created. Visitors walk through an herb garden and orangery to the formal rose garden. The mansion offers dramatic views of the Hudson Highlands and West Point Military Academy. More than 150 rose varieties are on display.

Clark Botanic Garden

Address 193 I.U. Willets Rd., Albertson, 11507
Phone (516) 484-2208
Website www.clarkbotanic.org
Hours 10 a.m. to 4 p.m. daily; closed most winter weekends
Fee No

This 12-acre living museum and educational facility has collections of native spring wildflowers, conifers, roses, perennials, wetland plants, herbs, medicinal plants, and rock gardens. The American Hemerocallis Society has recognized Clark as a Daylily Display Garden.

Colonial Garden

Address 7590 Court St., Elizabethtown, 12932
Phone (518) 873-6466
Website www.adkhistorycenter.org
Hours May–Oct., 10 a.m. to 5 p.m. daily
Fee Yes

Located behind the Adirondack History Center Museum, the garden displays formal beds filled with the colors of annuals, perennials, and native trees and shrubs. Maintained by the Essex County Adirondack Garden Club, the garden is patterned after Hampton Court in England and Colonial Williamsburg.

Cornell Plantations

Address 1 Plantations Rd., Ithaca, 14850
Phone (607) 255-2400
Website www.cornellplantations.org
Hours Sunrise to sunset, daily
Fee No

A welcome center opened in 2010 to guide visitors through the Plantations, a natural area at Cornell University. It includes the 150-acre F.R. Newman Arboretum, 25-acre botanical garden with 12 themed gardens, and a 4,000-acre natural area with trails for hiking.

Genesee County Village & Museum

Address 1410 Flint Hill Rd., Mumford, 14511
Phone (585) 538-6822
Website www.gcv.org
Hours Mid-May–mid-Oct., Tuesday–Friday, 10 a.m. to 4 p.m., Saturdays, Sundays, and holidays, 10 a.m. to 5 p.m.
Fee Yes

More than 40 buildings have been restored to create a nineteenth-century pioneer village, complete with a Village Center and a turn-of-the-century Main Street with live demonstrations. The gardens are planted to reflect the time, including a medicinal garden, formal garden, and a children's garden.

Hammond Museum and Japanese Stroll Garden

Address 28 Deveau Rd., North Salem, 10560
Phone (914) 669-5033
Website www.hammondmuseum.org
Hours May–Nov., Wednesday–Saturday, noon to 4 p.m.
Fee Yes

The Japanese Stroll Garden incorporates bends and curves to take visitors through the landscape without seeing everything at once. Visitors are invited to continue or stop and contemplate the view, sound, or fragrance, based on where plants are positioned.

Highland Botanical Garden and Lamberton Conservatory

Address 180 Reservoir Ave., Rochester, 14620
Phone (585) 753-7270
Website www.highlandparkconservancy.org
Hours Apr. 1–Oct. 31, daily, 7 a.m. to 11 p.m.; Nov. 1–Mar. 31, Monday–Thursday, 7 a.m. to 4 p.m., Friday–Sunday, 7 a.m. to 11 p.m.
Fee No for garden, yes for conservatory

Another Olmsted-designed park, the conservatory was built in 1911, but by 2006, had deteriorated significantly. Over the next few years, the conservatory was reconstructed with modern materials and replanted with tropical and other exotic plants. The Poet's Garden is a highlight of the landscape. Its lilac collection is world-renowned.

John P. Humes Japanese Stroll Garden

Address 347 Oyster Bay Rd., Mill Neck, 11765
Phone (516) 676-4486
Website www.locustvalley.com/japanese%20stroll%20garden.html
Hours Late Apr.–Oct., Saturday and Sunday, 11:30 a.m. to 4:30 p.m.
Fee Yes

Ambassador Humes built the 4-acre garden after returning from his assignment in Japan. It includes a shoin-dzukuri-style teahouse brought from Japan and placed on a lake in the garden. The serpentine paths in the garden offer variations of colors and textures. It has extensive use of moss and bamboo.

Innisfree Garden

Address 362 Tyrrel Rd., Millbrook, 12545
Phone (845) 677-8000
Website www.innisfreegarden.org
Hours Early May–mid-Oct., Wednesday–Friday, 10 a.m. to 4 p.m.,
Saturday, Sunday, and holidays, 11 a.m. to 5 p.m.
Fee Yes

This garden exemplifies the Chinese art of landscape architecture, which, like the Japanese, holds hidden views and surprises at each turn. Streams, waterfalls, terraces, retaining walls, rocks, and native plants enhance the scene. A focal point is the 40-acre glacial lake.

NEW YORK

Landis Arboretum

Address 174 Lape Rd., Esperance, 12066
Phone (518) 875-6935
Website www.landisarboretum.org
Hours Year-round, dawn to dusk
Fee No

Among the most important assets at this 548-acre arboretum with 8 miles of trails are two old-growth forests and a 500-year-old oak. Forty acres have been developed into display gardens, complete with trees, shrubs, and perennials from around the world.

Lasdon Park, Arboretum and Veterans Memorial

Address 2610 NY 35, Katonah, 10536
Phone (914) 864-7263
Website www.parks.westchestergov.com/index.php?option=com_content&task=view&id=1832&Itemid=4570
Hours Year-round, 8 a.m. to 4 p.m.; Veterans Museum, weekends only
Fee Yes

The arboretum includes a large azalea garden, yellow-blooming magnolias, lilacs, and pines. Deer, coyote, fox, and wild turkey call the grounds home. The Famous and Historic Tree Trail commemorates important events and people. The 1-acre Lasdon Memorial Garden has three areas—fragrance, formal, and synoptic. Woodlands, open meadows, and formal gardens round out the display.

Lyndhurst

Address 635 S. Broadway, Tarrytown, 10591
  Phone (914) 631-4481
Website www.hudsonvalley.org/content/view/18/48
  Hours Mid-Apr.–Oct., Tuesday– Sunday, 10 am. to 5 p.m.;
       Nov.–mid-Apr., weekends only, 10 a.m. to 4 p.m.
   Fee Yes

This 1838 Gothic Revival mansion overlooks the Hudson River. From the veranda, visitors can see the Tappan Zee Bridge. Evergreens recall the angular repetition of the home's Gothic roofline in a landscape that retains its nineteenth-century characteristics of scenic vistas and surprise views.

Madoo Conservancy

Address 618 Sagg Main St., Sagaponack, 11962
  Phone (631) 537-8200
Website www.madoo.org
  Hours May 15–Sept. 15, Friday and Saturday, noon to 4 p.m; other times by appointment
   Fee Yes

This is the home and garden of artist and author Robert Dash and is known for its punctuation of daring color amid myriad greens. The 2-acre plot embraces Tudor, High Renaissance, early Greek, and Oriental landscape influences. Look for surface patterns, windows, and doors in unlikely places.

Manitoga/The Russel Wright Design Center

Address 584 Rt. 9D, Garrison, 10524
Phone (845) 424-3812
Website www.russelwrightcenter.org
Hours May–Oct., only by reservation
Fee Yes

The 75-acre Manitoga preserves the legacy of designer Russel Wright, whose distinctive style signifies the 1930s, 1940s, and 1950s. He designed dinnerware, silverware, pottery, and furniture and worked in architecture and landscape architecture, all informed by his philosophy of informal living. The landscape is carefully designed to appear natural.

E. M. Mills Memorial Rose Garden

Address 736 Irving Ave., Thornden Park, Syracuse, 13210
Phone (315) 475-7244
Website www.syracuserosesociety.org
Hours Daily
Fee No

More than 3,800 roses adorn the garden, which started here in 1923 and is an All-America Rose Selections Display Garden. The Syracuse Rose Society maintains the garden. Not far from the rose garden is the lovely Lily Pond.

Montgomery Place

Address River Rd., Annandale-on-Hudson, 12504
Phone (845) 758-5461 or (914) 631-8200
Website www.hudsonvalley.org/content/view/16/46
Hours Year-round, 9 a.m. to 4 p.m. daily
Fee Grounds, no; grounds and house, yes

The nineteenth-century landscape is a mix of formal gardens and pathways for strolling. Perennial gardens, the serene ellipse, and the rough garden were created in the 1920s and 1930s. The 380-acre property is an intact experience of Hudson Valley estate living.

Mountain Top Arboretum

Address Rt. 23C and Maude Adams Rd., Tannersville, 12485
Phone (518) 589-3903
Website www.mtarboretum.org
Hours Year-round, dawn to dusk
Fee No

The arboretum is 2,400 feet above sea level in the rugged peaks of the Catskill Mountains. Native trees, shrubs, and wildflowers live with exotic transplants. It is difficult to push strollers and wheelchairs on most of the paths due to the soft surfaces.

Old Westbury Gardens

Address 71 Old Westbury Rd., Old Westbury, 11590
Phone (516) 333-0048
Website www.oldwestburygardens.org
Hours Beginning early Apr., weekends, 10 a.m. to 5 p.m.; late Apr.–Oct. 31, Wednesday–Monday
Fee Yes

Formal garden, allées, ponds, sculpture, gazebos, and border gardens with a strong English influence surround Westbury House, a Charles II–style mansion that was built in the early twentieth century. Several movies have been filmed here, including *Love Story* and *North by Northwest*.

Snug Harbor Cultural Center & Botanical Garden

Address 1000 Richmond Terrace, Staten Island, 10301
Phone (718) 448-2500 or (718) 285-6506
Website www.snug-harbor.org
Hours Grounds and park, dusk to dawn, daily
Fee Yes

The garden was founded in 1977 featuring a traditional English border. Today, this historic community's center is a White Garden, patterned after Vita Sackville-West's famous garden at Sissinghurst; a Secret Garden with a castle, maze, and walled garden; and the New York Chinese Scholar's Garden.

Sonnenberg Gardens & Mansion
State Historic Park

Address 151 Charlotte St., Canandaigua, 14424
Phone (585) 394-4922 or (585) 396-7433
Website www.sonnenberg.org
Hours May 1–29 and the day after Labor Day–Oct. 31, 9:30 a.m. to 4:30 p.m.;
Memorial Day–Labor Day, 9:30 a.m. to 5:30 p.m.
Fee Yes

These gardens are influenced by the owner's travels to Europe and Asia in the early twentieth century. There's a Japanese Garden, and Rose, Italian, and Blue and White Gardens. The Moonlight Garden has white- and silver-foliaged plants that bloom late in the day.

Stonecrop Gardens

Address 81 Stonecrop Lane, Cold Spring, 10516
Phone (845) 265-200
Website www.stonecrop.org
Hours Apr.–Oct., Monday–Friday and the first and third Saturdays, 10 a.m. to 5 p.m.;
May–Sept., open on Friday evenings until dusk
Fee Yes

Twelve acres of display gardens include a raised alpine stone bed, woodland and water gardens, and an English-style flower garden. There's also a conservatory and a display Alpine House. In spring, a collection of 50 types of dwarf bulbs bloom in beds in this Zone 5 garden.

Biltmore Estate

Address 1 Lodge St., Asheville, 28803
Phone (838) 225-1333 or (800) 411-3812
Website www.biltmore.com
Hours 8:30 a.m. to 6:30 p.m. daily
Fee Yes

George Vanderbilt's Biltmore was completed in 1895 and includes a French chateau surrounded by landscape and gardens designed by Frederick Law Olmsted. The Walled Garden is formal, emphasizing display rather than utility. The Italian Garden was designed as an outdoor room for entertaining with symmetrical pools and classical sculpture. Plan at least one full day at Biltmore. Admission includes Antler Hill Village and Winery. Still owned by a Vanderbilt family member, Biltmore remains an exquisite example of life in the Gilded Age.

North Carolina Botanical Garden

Address 100 Old Mason Farm Rd. Bypass, Chapel Hill, 27517
Phone (919) 962-0522
Website www.ncbg.unc.edu
Hours Weekdays, 8 a.m. to 5 p.m., Saturday, 9 a.m. to 6 p.m.,
Sunday, 1 p.m. to 6 p.m., weekends after Labor Day,
5 p.m. closing
Fee No

This botanical garden comprises nearly 800 acres, including 10 acres of display gardens and a number of natural areas in the Piedmont. Owned and operated by UNC at Chapel Hill, the garden's purpose is to research, catalog, and promote the native plants of North Carolina. Kids will love the Carnivorous Plant Collection of native Venus flytraps and other bug-eating plants. Other display gardens include the Native Plant Border, Native Water Gardens, Fern Collection, Herb Garden, Horticultural Therapy Garden, and Mountain and Coastal Plain/Sandhills habitats.

Sarah P. Duke Gardens

Address Duke University, 420 Anderson St., Durham, 27708
Phone (919) 684-3698
Website www.gardens.duke.edu
Hours 8 a.m. to dusk, daily
Fee No

The Duke Gardens sit at the heart of Duke University and were designed by Ellen Biddle Shipman, a renowned landscape designer. The gardens consist of four major areas on 55 acres: the original Terraces, Blomquist Garden of Native Plants, the Culberson Asiatic Arboretum, and the Doris Duke Center Gardens. Visitors can stroll 5 miles of allées and pathways throughout the gardens. The 36th latitude runs directly through the gardens and is marked with a plaque.

Wing Haven

Address 248 Ridgewood Ave., Charlotte, 28209
Phone (704) 331-0664
Website www.winghavengardens.com
Hours Tuesdays, 3 p.m. to 5 p.m., Wednesdays, 10 a.m. to noon, Saturdays, 10 a.m. to 5 p.m.
Fee Yes

Wing Haven encompasses the gardens of Elizabeth Lawrence, a renowned garden designer and author, and her neighbor, Elizabeth Clarkson, a garden and nature lover. Their passion resulted in modest, but exquisite gardens that were the talk of Charlotte for 30 years. Today, Clarkson's Wing Haven Gardens & Bird Sanctuary draws birds and other wildlife. Lawrence's garden fell into some disrepair, but sections have been restored and others are in process.

Airlie Gardens

Address 300 Arlie Rd., Wilmington, 28403
Phone (910) 798-7700
Website www.airliegardens.org
Hours Daily
Fee Yes

A majestic oak, which dates to 1545, and seasonal changes of the display gardens are big attractions to this historic property. So is the Minnie Evans Sculpture Garden and its Bottle Chapel with more than 4,000 glass bottles, metal sculptures, and mosaics.

Cape Fear Botanical Garden

Address 536 N. Eastern Blvd., Fayetteville, 28301
Phone (910) 486-0221
Website www.capefearbg.org
Hours Monday–Saturday, 10 a.m. to 5 p.m., Sunday, noon to 5 p.m.,
Thursday until 7 p.m. in summer
Fee Yes

The garden has 77 acres of preserved natural areas of the region's indigenous plants, trees, and wildlife. The gardens showcase more than 2,000 varieties of ornamental plants. The River Walk, Heritage Garden, Children's Garden, and Water Wise Garden provide unique educational experiences for young and old.

Daniel Boone Native Gardens

Address 651 Horn in the West Dr., Boone, 28607
Phone (828) 264-6390
Website www.danielboonegardens.org
Hours May 1–Oct., daily
Fee Yes

A collection of native trees, shrubs, and wildflowers offer a progression of bloom and color throughout the season. Featured are a bog garden, fern garden, rhododendron grove, rock garden, rock wishing well, vine-covered arbor, a pond by the historic Squire Boone Cabin, and grand vistas.

Daniel Stowe Botanical Garden

Address 6500 S. New Hope Rd., Belmont, 28013
Phone (704) 825-4490
Website www.dsbg.org
Hours 9 a.m. to 5 p.m. daily
Fee Yes

Daniel Jonathan Stowe, a retired textile executive, set aside nearly 400 acres of prime rolling meadows, woodland, and lakefront property. Since then, a Visitor Pavilion, Formal Display Gardens, a Willow Maze, Orchid Conservatory, and Perennial Gardens have been developed.

Elizabethan Gardens

Address 1411 National Park Dr., Manteo, 27954
Phone (252) 473-3234
Website www.elizabethangardens.org
Hours Daily
Fee Yes

This garden is on the Outer Banks and commemorates Sir Walter Raleigh's arrival. Highlights include a thatched, sixteenth-century-style gazebo, a Shakespeare Herb Garden, Queen's Rose Garden, Sunken Garden with antique Italian fountain, and a 400-year-old oak.

Gardens of Witherspoon

Address 3312 Watkins Rd., Durham, 37707
Phone (919) 489-4446 or (800) 643-0315
Website www.witherspoonrose.com
Hours Year-round
Fee No

Witherspoon installs and maintains rose gardens, but at this site, it has a showplace of more than 2,000 roses planted in landscape settings. It is a certified All America Rose Selection Public Garden and plays host to tours by garden clubs and gardening enthusiasts.

JC Raulston Arboretum

Address 4415 Beryl Rd., Raleigh, 27606
Phone (919) 515-3132
Website www.ncsu.edu/jcraulstonarboretum/index.php
Hours Apr.–Nov., 8 a.m. to 8 p.m. daily; Nov.–Mar., 8 a.m. to 5 p.m. daily
Fee No

The 8-acre arboretum at the University of North Carolina is known for its collection of redbuds, hollies, magnolias, oaks, and bamboo. Among the dozen garden themes is the Perennial Border, a spectacular 300-foot-long by 18-foot-deep bed, which contains thousands of plants.

Juniper Level Botanic Garden

Address 9241 Sauls Rd., Raleigh, 27604
Phone (919) 772-4794
Website www.juniperlevelbotanicgarden.org
Hours Several weekends a year, visit website for open dates
Fee No

This 6-acre display garden also serves as a research facility for Plant Delights Nursery, which is on the grounds. The botanical garden features plants that do well in the North Carolina climate, including several tropicals and agaves.

Ellen Mordecai Garden

Address 1 Mimosa St., Historic Park, Raleigh, 27604
Phone (919) 857-4364
Website www.raleighnc.gov/mordecai
Hours Sunrise to sunset, daily
Fee No

The garden is recreated from first hand descriptions of the Mordecai kitchen garden in the 1830s. It contains vegetables, herbs, and flowers that were grown through the nineteenth century and is arranged in squares of raised beds. Mordecai is the birthplace of President Andrew Johnson.

New Hanover County Co-Op Extension Arboretum

Address 6206 Oleander Dr., Wilmington, 28403
Phone (910) 798-7666
Website www.gardeningnhc.org
Hours Monday–Friday, 8 a.m. to 5 p.m.
Fee No

One of the highlights of this 7-acre coastal arboretum is the Ability Garden, used in a horticulture therapy program, which features raised beds, adaptive equipment, containers, and barrier-free space. There's also a Japanese Garden, Children's Garden, Perennial Border, Herb Garden, and Water Garden.

North Carolina Arboretum

Address 100 Frederick Law Olmsted Way, Asheville, 28806
Phone (828) 666-2492
Website www.ncarboretum.org
Hours Apr. 1– Oct. 31, 8 a.m. to 9 p.m.; Nov. 1–Mar. 31, 8 a.m. to 7 p.m.
Fee Yes, for parking; free the first Tuesday of the month

More than 65 acres of the 434-acre arboretum have display gardens or collections, including the Bonsai Exhibition Garden. This is one of the most scenic spots in the United States, right off the Blue Ridge Parkway in the Pisgah National Forest and southern Appalachian Mountains.

Sandhills Horticultural Gardens

Address 3395 Airport Rd., Pinehurst, 28374
Phone (910) 695-3882
Website www.sandhillshorticulturalgardens.com
Hours Dawn to sunset
Fee No

The sandhills divide the Piedmont from the coastal plains and are the remnants of a beach from a long-ago ocean. Sandhills Horticultural Gardens include a Japanese Garden, Children's Garden, Holy Garden, Fruit & Vegetable Garden, Annual Garden, Native Wetland Trail Garden, and the Sir Walter Raleigh Garden.

International Peace Garden

Address 10939 Hwy. 281, Dunseith, 58329
Phone (888) 432-6733; (701) 263-4390
Website www.peacegarden.com
Hours 24 hours a day
Fee Yes

The 2,300-acre garden has two lakes, hiking trails, waterfalls, wildflowers, and camping facilities. The display garden contains more than 150,000 flowers, and a meditation or therapeutic garden features the soothing sound of water. The garden shares its border with the International Peace Garden of Manitoba.

Fort Stevenson State Park Arboretum

Address 1252A 41st Ave., N.W., Garrison, 58540
Phone (701) 337-5576
Website www.ndparks.com/north-dakota-state-parks/
fort-stevenson-state-park.php
Hours Daily
Fee No

This new arboretum contains 50 native and exotic species of trees, shrubs, wildflowers, and grasses. The park is on Lake Sakakawea (Sacagawea) and includes the Lewis and Clark Expedition Trail. When the lake is low, petrified wood, leaf, and marine fossils can be observed, but not collected. The arboretum has native and non-native trees, shrubs, and grasses.

Myra Arboretum

Address U.S. Hwy. 2 and County Rd. 4A, Larimore, 58251
Phone (701) 343-2078
Website www.gfcounty.nd.gov/node/150
Hours Daily
Fee No

The 26-acre arboretum is in the same area as the Larimore Dam Recreation Area and Campground, a Grand Forks County park that opened in 1979. Known as the Upper Turtle Creek region, the arboretum demonstrates how 500 types of trees, shrubs, and perennials can work together in a landscape.

Cleveland Botanical Garden

Address 11030 East Blvd., Cleveland, 44106

Phone (216) 721-1600

Website www.cbgarden.org

Hours May 31–Labor Day, Tuesday–Saturday, 10 a.m. to 5 p.m.,
Sunday, noon to 5 p.m., Wednesday, 10 a.m. to 9 p.m.

Fee Yes

This lovely 10-acre site includes spectacular gardens and a conservatory. In the conservatory, visitors go from the desert of Madagascar to a Costa Rican rainforest, complete with butterflies. Outdoors, stroll through the Gateway Garden to the Perennial Border, Restorative Garden, and Terrace Garden. A Rose Garden, Topiary Garden, Herb Garden, Japanese Garden, and Woodland Garden are also featured. The Hershey Children's Garden, with its "scrounger" garden, cave, dwarf forests, worm bins, wheelchair-accessible tree house, and sensory-filled herb garden, is an exciting and enlightening destination.

Franklin Park Conservatory

Address 1777 E. Broad St., Columbus, 43203

Phone (614) 645-8733

Website www.fpconservatory.org

Hours 10 a.m. to 5 p.m. daily, Wednesday, until 8 p.m.

Fee Yes

The conservatory has 400 plant species and features a Victorian Palm House with more than 40 types of palms. The conservatory also has a collection by the glass artist Dale Chihuly. Outdoors are botanical and display gardens in the 88-acre Franklin Park.

Kingwood Center

Address 900 Park Ave. West, Mansfield, 44906
Phone (419) 522-0211
Website www.kingwoodcenter.org
Hours Apr.–Oct., 8 a.m. to 7 p.m., June–Aug., Thursday, until 8:30 p.m.; Mar. and Nov., 8 a.m. to 5 p.m.; Thanksgiving–Dec. 31, 11 a.m. to 5 p.m. daily, Thursday and Friday to 8 p.m.
Fee Yes

Open to the public since 1953, Kingwood Center is the 47-acre estate of a Mansfield industrialist. The grounds have seasonal displays in the garden, earning top marks for its spring tulip plantings. The Terrace Garden, opened in the 1990s, took Kingwood from being a display garden to integrated landscapes and gardens. Other features include peonies, irises, daylilies, and roses. The greenhouse has bird of paradise plants, an orangery, a succulent house, and an aquarium.

Stan Hywet Hall & Garden

Address 714 N. Portage Path, Akron, 44303
Phone (330) 836-5533 or (888) 836-5533
Website www.stanhywet.org
Hours Apr.–Dec., Tuesday–Saturday, 10 a.m. to 6 p.m.
Fee Yes

A reproduction of Corbin Conservatory, complete with the Gothic-patterned entryway and curved roof, opened in 2005. Ellen Biddle Shipman's English Garden is a crowd pleaser because of its color changes through the seasons. The Birch Allée Vista is an iconic scene, which leads to teahouses and an overlook of The Lagoons and the Cuyahoga Valley. The flowers from Great Garden are used in the Manor House year-round. The Gate Lodge is where Alcoholics Anonymous was founded.

Topiary Garden at Deaf School Park

Address 480 E. Town St., Columbus, 43215
Phone (614) 645-0197
Website www.topiarygarden.org
Hours Sunrise to sunset, daily
Fee No

A 7-acre park is known for its topiary interpretation of Georges Seurat's famous Post-Impressionist painting *A Sunday Afternoon on the Isle of La Grand Jatte*. Visitors stroll by yews and other evergreens that have been shaped into the characters and the scene from the iconic painting, including a topiary boat on a lake. The park also has beautifully landscaped walks, benches, picnic tables, and a Visitor's Center. The park was part of the former Ohio School for the Deaf, which dates to the early nineteenth century.

Cincinnati Zoo & Botanical Garden

Address 3400 Vine St., Cincinnati, 45220
Phone (513) 281-4700
Website www.cincinnatizoo.org
Hours 9 a.m. to 6 p.m. daily
Fee Yes

The gardens feature one of the largest annual displays in the Tri-State area, a perennial garden, ornamental grasses, trees and shrubs, tropicals, and deer-resistant plants. It has an extensive research program and collection of regional native plants, including trillium and lady slipper orchids.

Civic Garden Center of Greater Cincinnati

Address 2715 Reading Rd., Cincinnati, 45206
Phone (513) 221-0981
Website www.civicgardencenter.org
Hours Monday–Saturday, 9 a.m. to 4 p.m.
Fee No

The center is all about teaching people about gardening, including community garden development training. On the grounds you'll find a shade garden, herb garden, dwarf conifer garden, and butterfly gardens. Nearby is the Hauck Botanic Garden.

Cox Arboretum & Gardens

Address 6733 Springboro Rd., Dayton, 45449
  Phone (937) 434-9005
Website www.metroparks.org/Parks/CoxArboretum/Home.aspx
  Hours Monday–Friday, 8 a.m. to 5 p.m., Saturday–Sunday, 11 a.m. to 4 p.m.
    Fee No

Here you'll find Ohio's first native butterfly house along with significant natural areas, including cedar glades, mature woodlots, planted tall-grass prairie, and wetlands. More than 500 species of trees and shrubs are at the arboretum, which also has a children's maze.

Dawes Arboretum

Address 7770 Jacksontown Rd. SE, Newark, 43056
  Phone (800) 443-2937; (740) 323-2355
Website www.dawesarb.org
  Hours 7 a.m. to sunset, daily
    Fee No

Stroll through the All Seasons Garden, Azalea Glen, Cypress Swamp, Conifer Glen, Dutch Ford Wetlands, and Japanese Garden. The Children's Discovery Center and Daweswood House Museum are highlights. For a bird's-eye view of the arboretum, climb the Outlook Tower. The 1,800 acres include 8 miles of hiking trails.

Fellows Riverside Gardens

Address 123 McKinley Ave., Youngstown, 44509
Phone (330) 740-7116
Website www.millcreekmetroparks.com/ParksFacilities/
nbspnbspnbspnbspFellowsRiversideGardens/tabid/1409/Default.aspx
Hours Year-round, dawn to dusk, daily
Fee No

This 12-acre display garden features a landscape of remarkable beauty with diverse and colorful plants, roses of all classes, seasonal displays of annuals, perennials, flowering bulbs, and scenic vistas. At the Education and Visitor Center is the observation tower and Mill Creek Park museum.

Holden Arboretum

Address 9500 Sperry Rd., Kirtland, 44094
Phone (440) 946-4400
Website www.holdenarb.org
Hours 9 a.m. to 5 p.m. daily
Fee Yes

The arboretum has collections of false cypresses, arborvitaes, hedges, rhododendrons, conifers, lilacs, and viburnums. At Corning Lake, there's a duck blind for observing waterfowl. Lantern Court Gardens are open Monday through Friday, April through October, and are included in the admission to Holden.

Krohn Conservatory

Address 1501 Eden Park Dr., Cincinnati, 45202
Phone (513) 421-5707
Website www.cincinnatiparks.com/krohn-conservatory/index.shtml
Hours Tuesday–Sunday, 10 a.m. to 5 p.m.
Fee No, but fee for special shows

Built in 1933, the conservatory in Eden Park has a rainforest and collection of palms, orchids, bonsai, tropical, and desert plants. There are frequent exhibits of nature-related art and a butterfly show. Outdoors, display gardens are planted for the seasons.

Ohio State University Chadwick Arboretum & Learning Center

Address 2001 Fyffe Court (Howlett Hall), Columbus, 43210
Phone (614) 292-3848
Website www.chadwickarboretum.osu.edu
Hours Dawn to dusk, daily
Fee No

In the Lane Avenue Gardens, kids and grownups can walk a labyrinth patterned after the Chartres Cathedral labyrinth. At Arboretum North is a collection of buckeyes, native trees, prairie plants, and willows, as well as a rain garden.

Schoepfle Garden

Address 11106 Market St., Birmingham, 44816

Phone (440) 965-7237

Website www.metroparks.cc/reservation-schoepfle-garden.php

Hours First weekend in Apr.—end of Oct., 8 a.m. to 8 p.m. daily; last Sunday in Oct. to the end of Mar., 8 a.m. to 4:30 p.m.

Fee No

The musically themed Schoepfle Children's Garden blends plants, music, and nature. The 50-acre Natural Woodland site delights with its seasonal displays of native trees and shrubs along the Vermillion River. The Shade Garden has ferns and hostas, and the Formal Garden has a central path lined with colorful flowers.

Schedel Arboretum & Gardens

Address 19255 W. Portage River South Rd., Elmore, 43416

Phone (419) 862-3182

Website www.schedel-gardens.org

Hours Apr., Tuesday–Saturday, 10 a.m. to 4 p.m.; May 1–Oct. 31, Tuesday–Saturday, 10 a.m. to 4 p.m., Sundays, noon to 4 p.m.

Fee Yes

The gardens have 20,000 annuals, perennials, bonsai, cherry trees, a grove of dawn redwoods, bald cypress, a Japanese garden, a kitchen garden, and a rose garden. The 1800s Manor House has Archaic Bronze pieces (some 5,000 years old), jade, Oriental and Persian rugs, artwork, and collectibles.

Toledo Botanical Garden

Address 5403 Elmer Dr., Toledo, 43615
Phone (419) 536-5566
Website www.toledogarden.org
Hours Year-round, daily, daylight
Fee No

The Hosta Collection has been accredited by the North American Plant Collection Consortium, which recognizes the museum-like care with which these perennials are tended. Other features include the Color Garden, Pioneer Garden, Dahlia Garden, Grande Allée, and Art in the Garden.

Wegerzyn Gardens & Children's Discovery Garden

Address 1301 E. Siebenthaler Ave., Dayton, 45414
Phone (937) 277-6545
Website www.metroparks.org/Parks/WegerzynGarden/Home.aspx
Hours Apr. 1–Oct. 31, 8 a.m. to 10 p.m.; Nov. 1–Mar. 31, 8 a.m. to 8 p.m.; seasonal hours for Discovery Garden
Fee No

Ten themed gardens make up Wegerzyn Park, including a Victorian Garden and Federal Garden, reminiscent of eighteenth- and nineteenth-century American gardens, and elevated Plaza Gardens with vistas. A collection of disease-resistant roses forms the backbone of the display gardens.

Myriad Botanical Gardens

Address 301 W. Reno, Oklahoma City, 73102
Phone (405) 297-3995
Website www.myriadgardens.com
Hours Call ahead to confirm
Fee Grounds no; fee for Conservatory

The 17-acre Myriad Botanical Gardens is known for its Crystal Bridge Tropical Conservatory, a 224-foot-long cylindrical jungle graced with towering palm trees, exotic plantings, crashing waterfalls, and animal life. This living plant museum houses more than 1,000 specimens representing three tropical eco-zones, including the rainforest, desert, and island tropic zones. Plant collections include palms, cycads, gingers, bromeliads, orchids, euphorbias, and begonias. Outdoors, a children's garden, restaurant, dog release area, and multiple interactive water features provide hours of enjoyment, while the Meinders Gardens provides a botanical glimpse of the Oklahoma Ozarks. Look for special events and performances on the Water Stage and Grand Event lawn through the spring and summer.

Lendonwood Gardens

Address 1308 W. 13th St., Grove, 74345
  Phone (918) 786-2938
Website www.lendonwood.com
   Hours Year-round, daylight
      Fee Suggested donation

Lendonwood features the Display Garden, Oriental Garden with shade plants, Japanese Pavilion Garden and Koi Pond, English Terrace Garden with sunny beds and rhododendrons, and the American Backyard Garden, where plants thrive without much water.

Oklahoma Centennial Botanical Garden

Address 5323 W. 31st St., Tulsa, 74119
  Phone (918) 289-0330
Website www.ocbg.org
   Hours Early Apr.–late Oct., Saturdays, 9 a.m. to 4 p.m.
      Fee No

The 170-acre garden may be new, but its foundation is ancient—sandstone that is 400 million years old and clay at least 15 million. About 380 plant species have been identified on the land, including 100-year-old gnarled oaks.

Philbrook Museum of Art

Address 2727 S. Rockford Rd., Tulsa, 74114
 Phone (918) 749-7941
Website www.philbrook.org
 Hours Tuesday–Sunday, 10 a.m. to 5 p.m.; Thursday until 8:30 p.m.
 Fee Yes

The Italianate-influenced landscape design boasts a sensory garden, meditative niches made of plants, bridges, a sculpture walk, and a refurbished creek. The 1927 mansion houses art and changing exhibits. All trails are ADA accessible.

Woodward Park & Tulsa Garden Center

Address 2435 S. Peoria, Tulsa, 74114
 Phone (918) 746-5125
Website www.tulsagardencenter.com
 Hours Tuesday–Saturday, 8:30 a.m. to 4 p.m.
 Fee No

Woodward Park is the horticulture jewel box in Tulsa with its 1935 Municipal Rose Garden, the 1939 Anne Hathaway Herb Garden, and the Rock Gardens, one of which dates to 1930. The Garden Center houses garden and nature-related group meetings and an extensive horticultural library.

Oregon Garden

Address 879 W. Main St., Silverton, 97381

Phone (503) 874-8100

Website www.oregongarden.org

Hours May–Sept., 9 a.m. to 6 p.m. daily; Oct.–Apr., 10 a.m. to 4 p.m.

Fee Yes

The Oregon Garden features 25 themed gardens, including the A-Mazing Water Garden, Lewis and Clark Garden, Pet Friendly Garden, Tropical House, Ball Horticulture Trial Garden, Proven Winners Display Gardens, Sensory Garden, Train Garden, and the 400-year-old Signature Oak. A special tour of the gardens highlights sustainability efforts, including a green roof on a pump station. The Gordon House, designed by Frank Lloyd Wright, was moved to the garden in 2002. It is the only Wright-designed home in the Pacific Northwest open to the public.

Portland Japanese Garden

Address 611 SW Kingston Ave., Portland, 97205
Phone (503) 223-1321
Website www.japanesegarden.com
Hours Apr. 1–Sept. 30, Monday, noon to 7 p.m., Tuesday–Sunday,
10 a.m. to 7 p.m.; Oct. 1–Mar. 31, Monday, noon to 4 p.m.,
Tuesday–Sunday, 10 a.m. to 4 p.m.
Fee Yes

The Portland Japanese Garden is considered the most authentic Japanese garden outside of Japan. Situated on more than five acres nestled in the scenic west hills of Portland, the garden features five traditional styles: Flat Garden, Strolling Pond Garden, Tea Garden, Natural Garden, and Sand and Stone Garden. The purpose of the garden is to give visitors time to relax and refresh themselves by the pace of the walkways, views, textures, and sounds.

Azalea Park

Address Hwy. 101, Azalea Park Rd., Brookings, 97415
 Phone (541) 469-1100
Website www.brookings.or.us/parks%20and%20recreation/
azalea%20park/azalea%20park.htm
 Hours Daylight, daily
 Fee No

The fabulous native azaleas that still stand in the park were already here when Lewis and Clark wintered in Oregon in 1805–06. The gardens have been revitalized, creating the city's "crown jewel." It's home of *Capella By the Sea* by Elmo Williams, a wood and stone sculpture.

Crystal Springs Rhododendron Garden

Address 6015 SE 28th Ave., Portland, 97202
 Phone (503) 771-8386
Website www.portlandonline.com/parks/finder/index.cfm?PropertyID=27&action=ViewPark
 Hours Apr. 1–Sept. 30, 6 a.m. to 10 p.m. daily; Oct. 1–Mar. 31, 6 a.m. to 6 p.m.
 Fee Yes; free day after Labor Day–Feb.

The oldest rhododendron was planted here before 1917. Originally developed as a test garden, Crystal Springs suffered from a lack of security that made that impractical, so more than 2,500 rhododendrons, azaleas, and companion plants were planted. They provide color from spring through fall.

Hoyt Arboretum

Address 4000 SW Fairview Blvd., Portland, 97221
Phone (503) 865-8733
Website www.hoytarboretum.org
Hours 6 a.m. to 10 p.m. daily
Fee No

The 187-acre arboretum has more than 8,000 trees representing 1,000 species and 600 cultivars. Hydrangea, pittosporum, zelkova, and citrus make up some of the collections. Twenty-one ADA-accessible trails cover 12 miles through the property. There is something of interest every month.

Mount Pisgah Arboretum

Address 34901 Frank Parrish Rd., Eugene, 97405
Phone (541) 747-3817
Website www.mountpisgaharboretum.org
Hours Dawn to dusk, daily
Fee No

On the slopes of Mount Pisgah and the Willamette River, Mount Pisgah Arboretum has a 2-acre native plant garden, Oregon white oak savanna, river meadow, and riparian forest. The Visitor Center features "touch me" exhibits, reference books, and a working viewable beehive.

Chanticleer Garden

Address 786 Church Rd., Wayne, 19087
Phone (610) 687-4163
Website www.chanticleergarden.org
Hours Late Mar. to late Oct., Wednesday–Sunday,
10 a.m. to 5 p.m.; May–Labor Day, Fridays until 8 p.m.
Fee Yes

Known and revered as a pleasure garden, Chanticleer, a former estate, opened to the public in 1993. The house is densely planted with tropical plants, a popular selection for gardens throughout the property. A pathway of less than a mile takes visitors through a Tennis Court Garden, Gravel Garden, Teacup Garden, Minder Woods, Orchard, Cut Flower and Vegetable Garden, Pond Garden, and the Ruins. Sculpture and other art punctuate the landscape along with gorgeous views. The Ruins is one of the most dramatic gardens anywhere.

Longwood Gardens

Address 1001 Longwood Rd., Kennett Square, 19348
Phone (610) 388-1000
Website www.longwoodgardens.org
Hours Late May–Labor Day, Sunday–Thursday, 9 a.m. to 6 p.m.,
Friday–Saturday, 9 a.m. to 10 p.m.; winter hours vary
Fee Yes

Pierre S. du Pont, industrialist, conservationist, philanthropist, and great-grandson of the founder of E.I. du Pont de Nemours and Company, is credited with launching Longwood, one of the premier display gardens in the United States. The Conservatory, with 20 indoor gardens, and the 5-acre fountain garden are its heart. The fountains put on their show illuminated by 674 red, blue, green, yellow, and white lights keyed to music three nights a week. Longwood is a "must-see" destination of 1,077 truly gorgeous acres, of which 325 are open to the public.

Phipps Conservatory & Botanical Gardens

Address One Schenley Park, Pittsburgh, 15213
Phone (412) 622-6914
Website www.phipps.conservatory.org
Hours 9:30 a.m. to 5 p.m. daily, Friday until 10 p.m.
Fee Yes

Phipps Conservatory and Botanical Gardens, a great steel and glass Victorian greenhouse, has been inviting visitors to explore the beauty and mysteries of plants since 1893. Set amidst one of Pittsburgh's largest greenspaces, Schenley Park, Phipps Conservatory has evolved into one of the region's most vibrant, thriving cultural attractions, bringing fresh perspectives and artists into the historic glasshouse environment. The Phipps has been named one of the world's most energy-efficient and sustainable conservatories.

Bartram's Garden

Address 54th St. & Lindbergh Blvd., Philadelphia, 19143
Phone (215) 729-5281
Website www.bartramsgarden.org
Hours Early Apr.–early Dec, Tuesday–Thursday, 10 a.m. to 2 p.m.,
Friday–Sunday, 10 a.m. to 4 p.m.
Fee Yes

The eighteenth-century home and garden of John Bartram includes the furnished Bartram House, botanical garden, parkland, and wetland. John, American's first naturalist, explorer, and botanist, and his son, William, discovered the *Franklinia alatamaha* tree, named in honor of their friend Benjamin Franklin.

Bowman's Hill Wildflower Preserve

Address 1635 River Rd., New Hope, 18934
Phone (215) 862-2924
Website www.bhwp.org
Hours 8:30 a.m. to sunset, daily
Fee Yes

Native plants of the Delaware Valley region are center stage on this 134-acre preserve. There are more than 800 native plant species in naturalistic settings. This Bucks County preserve also is a favorite spot for birders.

Goodell Gardens & Homestead

Address 221 Waterford St. (Rt. 6N), Edinboro, 16412
 Phone (814) 734-6699
Website www.goodellgardens.org
 Hours May 1–Oct. 31, Wednesday–Sunday, 11 a.m. to 5 p.m.
 Fee Yes

The homestead dates to 1876, although some buildings are older. Carrie's Heritage Garden is historically significant in the diversity of cultivated plant species held, along with being a representative of American heirloom gardening. The rare Ben Franklin tree (*Franklinia alatamaha*) is on display.

Hershey Gardens

Address 170 Hotel Rd., Hershey, 17033
 Phone (717) 534-3492
Website www.hersheygardens.org
 Hours Early Apr.–Dec., various hours and days
 Fee Yes

Hershey Gardens opened in 1937, and through the years, a 3½-acre rose garden has blossomed into 23 acres of theme gardens, including a charming hands-on Children's Garden. In the summer, walk among 300 fluttering butterflies in the popular outdoor Butterfly House.

Lake Erie Arboretum at Frontier Park

Address 1650 Norcross Rd., Erie, 16505
Phone (814) 825-1700
Website www.leaferie.org
Hours Daily
Fee No

The arboretum holds more than 225 varieties of trees. It offers opportunities to stroll pathways through shade, flowering, and evergreen trees and over an urban stream. Become quiet and centered with a walk on the labyrinth.

Morris Arboretum

Address 100 E. Northwestern Ave., Philadelphia, 19118
Phone (215) 247-5777
Website www.morrisarboretum.org
Hours Apr.–Oct., 10 a.m. to 4 p.m. daily, weekends until 5 p.m.; June–Aug., Thursday, until 8:30 p.m.
Fee Yes

The 92-acre arboretum has 23 themed gardens and 16 sculptures amid tree collections, which include native magnolias, hollies, buckeyes, lacebark pines, and azaleas. The Garden Railway changes its theme each year, with villages made out of natural materials with meticulous detail.

Scott Arboretum

Address 500 College Ave., Swarthmore, 19081
Phone (610) 328-8025
Website www.scottarboretum.org
Hours Dawn to dusk, daily
Fee No

The Scott's collection features plants from the Delaware Valley and demonstrate how they can be used in residential settings. Collections of oaks, witch hazels, hydrangeas, conifers, crabapples, flowering cherries, roses, magnolias, hollies, and tree peonies have been registered with the North American Plant Collections Consortium.

Tyler Arboretum

Address 515 Painter Rd., Media, 19063
Phone (610) 566-9134
Website www.tylerarboretum.org
Hours 9 a.m. to 4 p.m. or 8 p.m. daily, depending on the season
Fee Yes

One of the oldest arboretums in the northeast United States, Tyler Arboretum contains 20 miles of hiking trails through woodlands, wetlands, and meadows. The Meadow Maze challenges puzzle-solving skills, and the Raptor's Roost gives the overhead view.

Blithewold Mansion, Gardens & Arboretum

Address 101 Ferry Rd. (Rt. 114), Bristol, 02809
Phone (401) 253-2707
Website www.blithewold.org
Hours Mid-Apr.–Columbus Day, Wednesday–Saturday,
10 a.m. to 4 p.m., Sundays, 10 a.m. to 3 p.m.
Fee Yes

Located on Narragansett Bay, Blithewold is one of the finest garden estates in New England. Blithewold includes several diverse gardens, specimen trees, and a 45-room English-style manor house filled with antiques and artwork, all chronicling the rich social history of one family over a span of more than 80 years. The landscape, designed in the late 1800s, has a sweeping lawn, which provides views of Narragansett Bay. The Display Garden features season-long flowers and color.

Green Animals Topiary Garden

Address 380 Corys Lane, Portsmouth, 02871
Phone (401) 847-1000
Website www.newportmansions.org/page10001214.cfm
Hours June 25–Oct. 10, 10 a.m.–5 p.m. daily
Fee Yes

One of the oldest topiary gardens in the country, more than 80 trees and shrubs have been pruned and trained into animals and geometric forms. There are also 35 gardens of flowers, vegetables, and fruit trees. A greenhouse produces plants used on the property.

Newport Mansions of the Preservation Society of Newport County

Address 424 Bellevue Ave., Newport, 02840
Phone (401) 847-1000
Website www.newportmansions.org
Hours Vary to season and property
Fee Yes

This organization fosters the preservation of 11 historic properties in Newport, appreciated for their architecture and landscapes. The properties are The Breakers, The Elms, Marble House, Rosecliff, Chateau-sur-Mer, Kingscote, Isaac Bell House, Green Animals, Hunter House, and Chepstow.

Brookgreen Gardens

Address 1931 Brookgreen Gardens Dr., Murrells Inlet, 29576
Phone (843) 235-6000
Website www.brookgreen.org
Hours 9:30 a.m. to 5 p.m. daily; mid-June–mid-Aug.,
Wednesday, Thursday and Friday, 9 p.m.
Fee Yes

Created in the 1930s on the site of former rice plantations, Brookgreen Gardens received the 2011 Heritage Tourism Award. It is home of some of the finest examples of American figurative sculpture, all placed in natural settings that preserve the area's native flora.

Middleton Place

Address 4300 Ashley River Rd., Charleston, 29414
Phone (843) 556-6020; (800) 782-3608
Website www.middletonplace.org
Hours 9 a.m. to 5 p.m. daily
Fee Yes

Henry Middleton started working on the gardens in 1741, making them a National Historic Landmark and home to America's oldest landscaped gardens. Designed in the classical European principles of the early eighteenth century, slaves built the terraces, walkways, artificial lakes, and long views to the river. Whether it's century-old camellias in winter, azaleas in spring, or kalmia, magnolias, crape myrtles, and roses in summer, the gardens were planned so there is something in bloom year-round.

South Carolina Botanical Garden

Address 102 Garden Trail, Clemson, 29634
Phone (864) 656-3405
Website www.clemson.edu/public/scbg
Hours Dawn to dusk, daily
Fee No

Located on the campus of Clemson University, the 295 acres hold a 70-acre arboretum, display gardens, natural landscapes, more than 400 camellias, and extensive collections of hollies, hydrangeas, magnolias, and native plants. Miles of nature trails wind through woodlands, meadows, fern gardens, and bogs. There is an award-winning sculpture collection. It is home to an official American Hosta Display Garden and has a butterfly garden. The Discover Center has a Reflection Garden, Vegetable Garden, and Garden Overlook.

Caldwell-Boylston Gardens/Lace House

Address 800 Richland St., Columbia, 29201
Phone (803) 737-2235
Website www.lacehouse.sc.gov/history/historyofcaldwellboylstongardens.htm
Hours Monday–Friday, 9:30 a.m. to 4:30 p.m.
Fee No

Located on the grounds of the South Carolina Governor's Mansion, the gardens date to the 1830s. The gardens are designed on three tiers: a boxwood parterre fronted by trees that are over 150 years old, open entertainment areas with a pergola draped in roses, and a cutting garden.

Edisto Memorial Gardens

Address 250 Riverside Dr., Orangeburg, 29115
Phone (803) 533-6020; (800) 545-6153
Website www.orangeburgsc.net/Quality/edisto.html
Hours Dawn to dusk, daily
Fee No

An All-America Rose Selections site, Edisto has 50 garden beds with more than 4,000 miniature, shrub, tea, climber, and other roses. The Horne Wetlands Park has a 2,600-foot boardwalk that juts into the Edisto River. There's also a butterfly garden and sensory garden.

Glencairn Garden

Address 725 Crest St., Rock Hill, 29730
Phone (803) 329-5620
Website www.cityofrockhill.com/dynSubPageSub.aspx?deptID=9999&pLinkID=
353&parentID=13
Hours Dawn to dusk, daily
Fee No

A couple of azaleas received as gifts in 1928, planted in a backyard, has grown into an 11-acre park with thousands of azaleas, camellias, crape myrtle, daylilies, and lily ponds. A Veterans Garden and tiered fountain opened recently.

Hampton Park

Address 30 Mary Murray Dr., Charleston, 29403
Phone (843) 724-7327
Website www.charlestonparksconservancy.org/our_parks/view_park/hampton_park/
Hours Daylight hours, daily
Fee No

This is Charleston's largest park and has the most extensively planted floral display beds. This area was once known as "The Ivory City" because temporary white palaces were built for an exposition in 1901. A sunken pool is all that remains from the exhibit.

Hatcher Garden & Woodland Preserve

Address 820 John B. White Sr. Blvd., Spartanburg, 29306
  Phone (864) 574-7724
Website www.hatchergarden.org
  Hours Daylight hours, daily
    Fee No

The Hatcher Garden & Woodland Preserve opened the Garden of Hope & Healing in 2011 for therapeutic programs and other mental health–related activities. A butterfly garden, adorned with a giant monarch caterpillar, draws young and old to gardens filled with the winged beauties.

Magnolia Plantation and Gardens

Address 3550 Ashley River Rd., Charleston, 29414
  Phone (800) 367-3517; (843) 556-1013
Website www.magnoliaplantation.com
  Hours Mar.–Oct., 9 a.m. to 4:30 p.m. daily. Call for winter hours.
    Fee Yes

A recent cultural landscape report says Magnolia has the oldest picturesque garden in the United States. With a 300-year history in horticulture, it was the first private garden to be opened to the public. The home is also open for tours. The camellia and azalea collections are noteworthy.

McKennan Park

Address 400 East 26th St., Sioux Falls, 57105
Phone (605) 367-8222
Website www.siouxfalls.org/Information/history/park_history/
mckennan.aspx
Hours 5 a.m. to 10 p.m. daily
Fee No

After several decades of disrepair, neighbors and the city have renovated key sections of McKennan Park, considered the jewel of the park system. A bandshell was renovated, a new wading pool installed, and reproductions of statues were placed. The park in this historic neighborhood has never been touched by a plow and the prairie remains the same as it was. It has now been surrounded by the city. Display gardens feature seasonal changes and perennial borders.

McCrory Gardens & Arboretum

Address 6th Street and 22nd Ave., Brookings, 57106
Phone (605) 688-5137
Website www.sdstate.edu/hflp/mccrory/index.cfm
Hours Dawn to dusk, daily
Fee No

There are 20 acres of gardens and 46 acres of arboretum operated by South Dakota State University for educational and research purposes for public displays. There are 14 themed gardens, including a children's maze, rose garden, and the Centennial Prairie Garden.

Memorial Park Rose Gardens

Address 5th & Omaha St., Rapid City, 57701
Phone (605) 394-4167
Website www.rcgov.org/Parks-and-Recreation/memorial-park.html
Hours Daily
Fee No

The garden commemorates the 238 victims of a devastating flood in June 1972. The rose gardens are located on the west side of Memorial Park next to the Civic Center. This All-America Rose Selections Garden with 1,200 roses represents 120 different varieties of hybrid tea, grandiflora, and floribunda roses.

Cheekwood Botanical Garden & Museum of Art

Address 1200 Forrest Park Dr., Nashville, 37205

Phone (615) 356-8000

Website www.cheekwood.org

Hours Tuesday–Saturday, 9:30 a.m. to 4:30 p.m., Sunday, 11 a.m. to 4:30 p.m.

Fee Yes

The former estate of the Cheek family, which started the Maxwell House Coffee brand, holds the Shomu-en Japanese garden, herb garden, two perennial borders, a color garden, water garden, seasonal garden, and an award-winning wildflower garden. Each garden has a special purpose presenting a particular group of plants or garden style. The Carell Woodland Sculpture Trail features art integrated into a reclaimed woodland. Exotic species were replaced with native species, including hickory, red cedar, oak, ash, and persimmon.

Memphis Botanic Garden

Address 750 Cherry Rd., Memphis, 38117
Phone (901) 576-4100
Website www.memphisbotanicgarden.com
Hours Monday–Sunday, 9 a.m. to 6 p.m., Sunday, 11 a.m. to 6 p.m.,
Monday–Saturday, 9 a.m. to 4:30 p.m., Sunday,
11 a.m. to 4:30 p.m.
Fee Yes

Twenty-four separate gardens adorn the grounds of the botanic garden, which also includes My Big Backyard children's garden with original nature-related artwork by mid-South artists. The first garden was the Tennessee Bicentennial Iris Garden. One of the newest is the Herb Garden, located next to the iris garden. At the Hyde & Seek Prehistoric Plant Trail, families can learn about prehistoric plants. The Four-Seasons garden display beds provide seasonal progressions of color that flank a long, low fountain.

Dixon Gallery & Gardens

Address 4339 Park Ave., Memphis, 38117
  Phone (901) 761-5250
Website www.dixon.org
  Hours Tuesday–Friday, 10 a.m. to 4 p.m., Saturday, 10 a.m. to 5 p.m.,
        Sunday, 1 p.m. to 5 p.m.
    Fee Yes, but with several free or low-cost days and times

Carved out of a Tennessee woodland, the gardens contain fine old trees, and natural and man-made vistas all designed with an English influence. Large, open spaces and views are adjacent to smaller, more intimate gardens. The gallery hosts a changing series of art exhibits.

Knoxville Botanical Garden and Arboretum

Address 2743 Wimpole Ave., Knoxville, 37914
  Phone (865) 862-8717
Website www.knoxgarden.org
  Hours Sunrise to sunset, daily
    Fee No

Visitors can wander through a bamboo forest, cedars of Lebanon trees, a perennial border, past charming, round stone buildings, and make a stop on the Eastern Tennessee Quilt Trail. Once a thriving nursery and Knoxville's longest-running business, the gardens are surrounded by beautiful stone walls.

Dallas Arboretum & Botanical Gardens

Address 8525 Garland Rd., Dallas, 75218
  Phone (214) 515-6500
Website www.dallasarboretum.org
  Hours 9 a.m. to 5 p.m. daily
    Fee Yes

There are 15 display gardens, groves of pecan trees, magnolias, crape myrtles, cherry trees, and azaleas. Set to open in 2012 is the Children's Adventure Garden, with 15 indoor and outdoor classrooms, a wetland walk, skywalk, and a look at the life of plants. The Lay Ornamental Garden is a 2-acre Texas cottage garden with hundreds of perennials and a falling water curtain against native limestone walls. Bronze wildlife figures are nestled in this garden too.

Lady Bird Johnson Wildflower Center

Address 4801 La Crosse Ave., Austin, 78739

Phone (512) 232-0100

Website www.wildflower.org

Hours Tuesday–Saturday, 9 a.m. to 5:30 p.m.,
Sunday, noon to 5:30 p.m.

Fee Yes

Lady Bird Johnson and actress Helen Hayes founded a research center to protect and preserve North American native plants in 1982. Now renamed for the former First Lady, the center is part of the University of Texas and one of the most respected resources for native plants in the United States. From the Entrance Trail and Garden, through the Meadows, Wetlands, and Courtyard, visitors are immersed in the beauty and sustainability of native perennials, annuals, trees, and shrubs.

Zilker Botanical Garden

Address 2220 Barton Springs Rd., Austin, 78704
Phone (512) 477-8672
Website www.ci.austin.tx.us/zilker
Hours 7 a.m. to 5:30 p.m. (7 p.m. during DST)
Fee Yes, for special events

Zilker Botanical Garden features several signature gardens including the Rose Garden, Green Garden, Taniguchi Japanese Garden, Butterfly Trail, Children's Garden, Pioneer Settlement, and the Hartman Prehistoric Garden where dinosaur tracks were discovered and preserved in 1992. Specialty gardens include the Herb Garden, Cactus and Succulent Garden, Daylily Garden, Iris Garden, Bamboo Grove, and other seasonal gardens. Annual garden shows and sales include the Cactus and Succulent Show, Bamboo Show, Iris Show, Green Garden Fest, and the Zilker Garden Festival. Other events and activities are offered seasonally.

Beaumont Botanical Gardens and Warren Loose Conservatory

Address 6088 Babe Zaharias Dr., Beaumont, 77705
Phone (409) 842-3135
Website www.beaumontbotanicalgardens.org
Hours Daily, daylight hours for garden; Conservatory, Wednesday–Friday, 10 a.m. to 2 p.m., Saturday, 10 a.m. to 5 p.m., Sunday, 1 p.m. to 5 p.m.
Fee Free for gardens, fee for Conservatory

The 23-acre garden is inside Tyrell Park and its 500 shade trees. Garden collections include bromeliads, herbs, antique and modern roses, azaleas, and native plants. A pond with a stone waterfall has turtles, koi, and ducks waiting for visitors to feed them.

Chandor Gardens

Address 711 W. Lee Ave., Weatherford, 76086
Phone (817) 613-1700
Website www.ci.weatherford.tx.us/index.aspx?NID=170
Hours Monday–Friday, 9 a.m. to 5 p.m., Saturday, 9 a.m. to 3 p.m., Sunday, noon to 4 p.m.
Fee Yes

The 3½-acre Chandor Gardens, with Chinese architecture and a formal English garden, lead visitors on a path of beauty. It is a member of the Gardens for Peace Community, which unites gardens around the world as universal places of meditation and symbols for peace.

Clark Gardens Botanical Park

Address 567 Maddux Rd., Weatherford, 76088
Phone (940) 682-4856
Website www.clarkgardens.org
Hours Monday–Saturday, 7:30 a.m. to 6 p.m., Sunday, 10 a.m. to 5 p.m.
Fee Yes

Collections at the garden include native spring wildflowers, conifers, roses, perennials, wetland plants, rock garden plants, herbs, butterfly plants, and medicinal plants. Clark Botanic Garden is an official Daylily Garden by the American Hemerocallis Society.

Fort Worth Botanic Garden

Address 3220 Botanic Garden Blvd., Fort Worth, 76107
Phone (817) 871-7686
Website www.fwbg.org
Hours 8 a.m. to dusk, garden center and conservatory hours vary
Fee Yes

The Texas Native Forest Boardwalk treks through treetops and has interactive boxes to listen for sounds of birds and other wildlife. The Fragrance Garden, with scent pleasing "touch-me" plants, has a fountain, and the Japanese Garden has a large pond of koi that like to be fed.

TEXAS

Hermann Park Conservancy

Address 6201-A Hermann Park Dr., Houston, 77030
Phone (713) 524-5876
Website www.hermannpark.org
Hours 6 a.m. to 11 p.m.
Fee No

The conservancy oversees Hermann Park, preserving and conserving this greenspace that is in the heart of Houston. Outside the Garden Center are beds with 2,000 roses and an international sculpture garden. Visitors can take a train ride through the park or a paddleboat on the lake.

Mercer Arboretum & Botanic Gardens

Address 22306 Aldine Westfield Rd., Humble, 77338
Phone (281) 443-8731
Website www.hcp4.net/mercer
Hours 8 a.m. to 5 p.m.
Fee No

Aldine Westfield Road divides the arboretum and botanic gardens' 325 acres. On the east, there are 20 acres of planted and maintained gardens and hiking trails. The arboretum on the west side has a hickory bog, boardwalk, cypress swamp, large picnic area, and miles of trails.

San Antonio Botanical Garden

Address 555 Funston Place, San Antonio, 78209
Phone (210) 207-3250 or TTY (210) 207-3097
Website www.sabot.org
Hours 9 a.m. to 5 p.m.
Fee Yes

The Texas Native Trail encompasses three distinctive ecological regions with scenes enhanced by reconstructed early Texas homes. The Conservatory has exhibits depicting deserts to rainforests. Older flower varieties can be found in the Old Fashioned Garden, one of four formal or display gardens.

South Texas Botanical Gardens & Nature Center

Address 8545 S. Staples, Corpus Christi, 78413
Phone (361) 852-2100
Website www.stxbot.org
Hours 8 a.m. to 6 p.m. daily; June 1–Labor Day, 8 a.m. to 7 p.m.
Fee Yes

Among the gardens' collections are bromeliads, plumeria, and orchids, which number more than 2,000. On the flyway for migrating birds, hummingbirds will find their own garden. Climb the birding tower or trek onto the Wetland Awareness Boardwalk.

TEXAS

Tyler Municipal Rose Garden

Address 420 Rose Park Dr., Tyler, 75702
Phone (903) 597-3130
Website www.texasrosefestival.com/museum/garden.htm
Hours Monday–Friday, 9 a.m. to 4:30 p.m., Saturday, 10 a.m. to 4:30 pm.,
Sunday, 1:30 p.m. to 4:30 p.m. Closed Monday, Nov.–Feb.
Fee Yes

Roses are tested for their vigor, flowers, disease resistance, and other factors for at least two years at an All-America Rose Selection Garden. The 14-acre garden includes old-fashioned, or heritage, roses and a sensory garden. The meditation garden near the reflecting pool is another a favorite spot.

Umlauf Sculpture Garden & Museum

Address 605 Robert E. Lee Rd., Austin, 78704
Phone (512) 445-5582
Website www.umlaufsculpture.org
Hours Wednesday–Friday, 10 a.m. to 4:30 p.m., Saturday–Sunday, 1 p.m. to 4:30 p.m.
Fee No

More than 200 statues are placed on the grounds of the Umlauf Garden and Museum, which also is the home and studio of the artist. The artist thinks visitors are more comfortable with art outdoors rather than having to stand still and be quiet.

Red Butte Garden and Arboretum

Address 300 Wakara Way, Salt Lake City, 84108
Phone (801) 585-0556
Website www.redbuttegarden.org
Hours Daily, hours vary according to season
Fee Yes

About 24 gardens or natural areas are scattered through the garden and arboretum, including The Children's Garden with a snake fountain. There's a Fragrance Garden, Courtyard, Herb Garden, Orangery, Four Seasons Garden, Flower Walk, and Wildflower Meadow. The Water Pavilion has three ponds and a waterfall garden. The arboretum and garden specialize in the study of Intermountain West plant species and habitats. Among the collections are viburnum, grasses, artemisia, conifer, daylily, and lavender.

International Peace Gardens at Jordan Park

Address 1000 S. 900 West, Salt Lake City, 84104
Phone (801) 972-7860
Website www.internationalpeacegardens.org
Hours 7:30 a.m. to 11 p.m. daily
Fee No

Various garden plots have plants representing many cultures. The gardens are decorated with flags and other symbols from 26 different countries. The Gardens are a repository of information and history of peace gardens. A copy of the Little Mermaid statue is located in the park.

Utah Botanical Center

Address 725 Sego Lily Dr., Kaysville, 84037
Phone (801) 593-8969
Website www.utahbotanicalcenter.org
Hours Dawn to dusk, daily
Fee Yes

The UBC demonstrates and practices sustainable principles, which can significantly reduce impact on the land and other valuable resources. Demonstrations use environmentally friendly products, recycled materials, and water-conserving landscapes. Sustainable home landscaping, wetland restoration, habitat creation, and water quality enhancement are all highlighted on public open space.

Hildene

Address 940 Hildene Rd., Manchester, 05254
Phone (800) 578-1788; (802) 362-1788
Website www.hildene.org
Hours 9:30 a.m. to 4:30 p.m. daily
Fee Yes

This was the summer home of Robert Todd Lincoln, the oldest son of Abraham and Mary Lincoln. The property stayed in the family until 1975, when it was purchased by the Friends of Hildene in 1978, which began the restoration process. The gardens, designed by an apprentice of Frederick Law Olmsted, include a Formal Garden, where 1,000 peonies bloom in spring, a Kitchen and Cutting Garden, and Meadows. The Georgian Revival–style home has 24 rooms and a 1,000 pipe organ.

Park-McCullough

Address 1 Park St., North Bennington, 05257
Phone (802) 442-5441
Website www.parkmccullough.org
Hours Mid-May–mid-Oct., 10 a.m. to 4 p.m. daily; Nov.–Apr., group tours by appointment
Fee Yes

Most of the historic buildings remain on the 600-acre estate, including an elaborate carriage barn with historic carriages. It also serves as a venue for concerts, theater, and other special events. The beautiful grounds include the rose garden, which is considered quite picturesque.

Shelburne Farms

Address 1611 Harbor Rd., Shelburne, 05482
Phone (802) 985-8686
Website www.shelburnefarms.org
Hours Early May–mid-Oct., 9 a.m. to 5:30 p.m. daily; winter, 10 a.m. to 5 p.m.
Fee Yes

Shelburne Farms is a 1,400-acre working farm and National Historic Landmark on the shores of Lake Champlain. Its mission is to cultivate a conservation ethic for a sustainable future. Casual visitors may enjoy the walking trails, children's farmyard, inn, restaurant, property tours, and special events.

Bon Air Park Rose Garden

Address 850 N. Lexington St., Arlington, 22205
Phone (703) 228-6525
Website www.arlingtonva.us/departments/parksrecreation/
scripts/parks/BonAirPark.aspx
Hours Sunrise to half hour after sunset
Fee No

Bon Air Park features the Memorial Rose Garden, one of the largest rose gardens along the Atlantic seaboard. The Arlington Rose Foundation wanted to create a garden to honor those who serve their country. More than 135 varieties and 2,500 plants represent all types of roses. There are also display gardens for azaleas. The Shade Garden features low-maintenance plants, and the sun garden has a color progression from April through October. A collection of small flowering ornamental trees rounds out the gardens.

Lewis Ginter Botanical Garden

Address 1800 Lakeside Ave., Richmond, 23228

Phone (804) 262-9887

Website www.lewisginter.org

Hours 9 a.m. to 5 p.m., extended hours in summer

Fee Yes

More than 50 acres are planted with a dozen themed gardens, including a Children's Garden, Healing Garden, Sunken Garden, Wetland, Rose Garden, Asian Valley, and Victorian Garden. A domed conservatory—the only one of its kind in the Mid-Atlantic states—has regularly changing displays of orchids and tropical plants. Ginter was influenced by Victorian design and by the neat and orderly landscape he observed in Australia in 1888. Among the gardens' plant collections are Japanese water iris, lotus, osmanthus, and ornamental pines.

Pavilion Gardens

Address 400 Ray C. Hunt Dr., Charlottesville, 22904
Phone (434) 924-4524
Website www.virginia.edu/uvatours/gardens/gardensHistory.html
Hours Daily
Fee No

At the University of Virginia, founder Thomas Jefferson embraced "groves of academe," which links gardens to the contemplative and scholarly life. Ten numbered gardens showcase many plants that Jefferson grew in his gardens at Monticello, as well as ones recommended by eighteenth-century gardeners. The Pavilion Gardens provide both a place in which to study and a subject of study. UNESCO named the university's grounds a World Heritage Site.

VIRGINIA

Bryan Park Azalea Gardens

Address 4308 Hermitage Rd., Richmond, 23227
Phone (804) 780-5733
Website www.friendsofbryanpark.org
Hours Sunrise to sunset, daily
Fee No

The Azalea Garden was started in 1952 by a former Richmond Recreation and Parks Superintendent of Grounds and Structures. Over an almost 15-year span, he and others planted 450,000 azaleas (50 different varieties) in approximately 76 separate beds.

Colonial Williamsburg

Address Colonial Williamsburg, 23187
Phone (757) 229-1000
Website www.history.org
Hours 9 a.m. to 5 p.m. daily
Fee Yes

Colonial Williamsburg is known for its cool green spaces, tidy flower gardens, fenced pastures, trimmed boxwoods, and big shade trees. Historians and horticulturists have combined historically accurate native plants with exotics that tolerate the hot humid summers to create the gardens and green spaces. Christmas has extensive seasonal displays.

Green Spring Gardens

Address 4603 Green Spring Rd., Alexandria, 22312
Phone (703) 642-5173
Website www.fairfaxcounty.gov/parks/gsgp
Hours Monday–Saturday, 9 a.m. to 4:30 p.m., Sunday, noon to 4:30 p.m.
Fee No

The gardens were designed by Beatrix Farrand and include boxwood hedges, roses, and perennial borders. Gardens featuring a wide variety of trees, shrubs, vines, perennials, annuals, bulbs, and vegetables provide ideas and inspiration for the home gardener.

Hahn Horticulture Garden

Address 200 Garden Lane, Virginia Tech, Blacksburg, 24061
Phone (540) 231-5783
Website www.hort.vt.edu/hhg
Hours Dawn to dusk, daily
Fee No

The garden, about six acres on the campus of Virginia Tech University, was started in 1984 by the horticulture faculty as a learning resource and demonstration garden. Features include perennial borders, water gardens, shade gardens, meadow gardens, and the Peggy Lee Hahn Garden Pavilion.

VIRGINIA

Maymont

Address 2201 Shields Lake Dr., Richmond, 23220
Phone (804) 358-7166
Website www.maymont.org
Hours 10 a.m. to 5 p.m. daily; mid-Mar.–early Nov., 10 a.m. to 7 p.m.
Fee Yes

This Victorian country estate with a Romanesque mansion has survived from the 1880s intact, with a life today as a public park and museum. The magnificent grounds with bluffs, outcroppings, and ravines feature an Italian Garden, Japanese Garden, Arboretum, and specialty gardens showcasing plants such as herbs and daylilies. The Butterfly Trail is sure to please.

Monticello

Address 931 Thomas Jefferson Parkway, Charlottesville, 22902
Phone (434) 984-9822
Website www.monticello.org
Hours Daily, daylight, hours vary by date
Fee Yes

Monticello is the estate of Thomas Jefferson, an avid gardener and plants-man as well as the framer of the U.S. Constitution and third president of the United States. His gardens were botanical showpieces and the source of food. He grew 220 varieties in a 1,000-foot-long vegetable bed and 170 fruit varieties in orchards. The Thomas Jefferson Center for Historic Plants was formed in 1987 to collect, preserve, distribute historic varieties, and promote overall appreciation of the evolution of garden plants.

Mount Vernon Estate & Gardens

Address 3200 Mount Vernon Memorial Hwy., Mount Vernon, 22309
Phone (703) 780-2000
Website www.mountvernon.org
Hours Apr.–Aug. 8 a.m. to 5 p.m.; Mar., Sept. and Oct., 9 a.m. to 5 p.m.; Nov.–Feb., 9 a.m. to 4 p.m.
Fee Yes

America's first president was an avid gardener and installed a pleasure garden in the Upper Garden. The Lower Garden's kitchen garden still looks like it would have in the late 1700s with rows of vegetables and fruits. Washington's "little garden" is where he experimented with different plants and seeds.

Norfolk Botanical Garden

Address 6700 Azalea Garden Rd., Norfolk, 23518
Phone (757) 441-5830
Website www.norfolkbotanicalgarden.org
Hours Oct. 16–Mar., 9 a.m. to 5 p.m.; Apr.–Oct. 15, 9 a.m. to 7 p.m.
Fee Yes

More than 30 themed gardens are in the garden. Some gardens focus on a single plant, such as hydrangeas or roses, while others look at a plant from a specific region, such as Virginia. Still others offer ideas home-owners can use in their own gardens.

River Farm

Address 7931 E. Boulevard Dr., Alexandria, 22308
Phone (703) 768-5700; (800) 777-7931
Website www.ahs.org/river_farm
Hours Monday–Friday, 9 a.m. to 5 p.m.; Apr.–late Sept., Saturday, 9 a.m. to 1 p.m.
Fee No

Once owned by George Washington, River Farm is the headquarters of the American Horticultural Society. A spectacular feature of the property is the Andre Bluemel Meadow. For decades, the 4-acre expanse was all lawn. In the mid-2000s, more than 100,000 native perennials, annuals, and grasses replaced the lawn.

Woodrow Wilson Birthplace and Gardens

Address 18 N. Coalter St., Staunton, 24401
Phone (540) 885-0897
Website www.woodrowwilson.org
Hours Nov.–Feb., Monday–Saturday, 10 a.m. to 4 p.m., Sunday, noon to 4 p.m.;
Mar.–Oct., Monday–Saturday, 9 a.m. to 5 p.m., Sunday, noon to 5 p.m.
Fee Yes

A Victorian restoration of the gardens, suitable to the 1846 construction date of the house, included two terraces. The lower one features boxwood-lined bowknot beds. In 1990, a garden walkway was added to connect all of the property, including the museum, library, and birthplace.

Dunn Gardens

Address	13533 Northshire Rd. NW, Seattle, 98177
Phone	(206) 362-0933
Website	www.dunngardens.org
Hours	Guided tours only with reservation, Apr.–Oct. except Aug.
Fee	Yes

In 1916, the Olmsted Brothers firm designed the landscape, which remains intact today with its characteristic curvilinear drive and footpaths. The edge of the Great Lawn follows the plan, which preserved many of the property's existing fir trees and plants, and the deciduous trees planted by the owner provide visual contrast to the south. The woodland gardens include rhododendrons, specimen flowering trees, and woodland plants such as erythroniums and trilliums, sited beneath a canopy of fir and deciduous trees that remain from the original gardens.

Manito Park and Botanical Gardens

Address 1702 S. Grand Blvd., Spokane, 99203

Phone (509) 625-6200

Website www.manitopark.org

Hours Daily in summer, 4 a.m. to 11 p.m.; daily in winter, 5 a.m. to 10 p.m.

Fee No

Spread over 98 acres, Manito Park was first established in 1904 and is best known for its five fantastic gardens. The Gaiser Conservatory shelters brilliantly colored tropical plants. Outdoor gardens like the Nishinomiya Japanese Garden, Duncan Garden, Lilic Garden, and Rose Hill display plants ranging from 150 rose varieties and lilacs to water-based plant species. The Ferris Perennial Garden is an ever-changing palette of color from spring to fall. With 300 varieties of plants, the vastness of colors, textures, flowers, and scents is beautiful.

Bellevue Botanical Garden

Address 12001 Main St., Bellevue, 98005
Phone (425) 452-2750
Website www.bellevuebotanical.org
Hours Dawn to dusk, daily
Fee No

The garden features a Northwest Perennial Alliance Border, Waterwise Garden, Yao Garden, Alpine Rock Garden, and summer displays of dahlias and fuchsias. As natural and man-made vistas of color and greenery change, they delight the eye regardless of the season or weather.

Bloedel Reserve

Address 7571 NE Dolphin Dr., Bainbridge Isle, 98110
Phone (206) 842-7631
Website www.bloedelreserve.org
Hours Tuesday–Sunday, 10 a.m. to 4 p.m.; June–Aug., Tuesday–Saturday, 10 a.m. to 7 p.m., Sunday, 10 a.m. to 4 p.m.
Fee Yes

The French country-style home, converted to a Visitor Center, overlooks Puget Sound. The 150-acre property is dense Northwest forest. A tall trestle bridge gives a bird's-eye look down at a year-round stream. Several gardens include a wetlands boardwalk that takes visitors to a bog with singing frogs and carnivorous plants.

Evergreen Arboretum and Gardens

Address 145 Alverson Blvd., Everett, 98201
Phone (425) 257-8597
Website www.evergreenarboretum.com
Hours Dawn to dusk, daily
Fee No

When you step through the Little and Lewis blue entrance columns, you are transported to a place of beauty and peace. Trees, shrubs, perennial gardens, a rock garden, and a Japanese maple walk, plus sculptures and a fountain work together to form a unique destination.

Kruckeberg Botanic Garden

Address 20312 15th Ave. NW, Shoreline, 98177
Phone (205) 546-1281
Website www.kruckeberg.org
Hours Sept. 23–Mar. 24, Friday–Sunday, 10 a.m. to 3 p.m.; Mar. 25–Sept. 22, 10 a.m. to 5 p.m.
Fee No

This 4-acre public garden contains 2,000 species of Pacific Northwest native plants and unusual exotics set in a naturalistic wooded setting. Plants include conifers, hardwoods, rhododendrons, magnolias, ferns, and groundcovers. Several trees are the largest or most rare in the state.

Lake Wilderness Arboretum

Address 22520 SE 248th, Maple Valley, 98038
Phone (425) 413-2572 or (206) 366-2125
Website www.lakewildernessarboretum.org
Hours Dawn to dusk, daily
Fee No

Begun in the mid-1960s, volunteers worked with the city to carve out 40 acres and create an arboretum. It is maintained to preserve, protect, and display Northwest ecosystems, as well as cultivated landscapes. There are a variety of themed gardens.

Lakewold Gardens

Address 12317 Gravelly Lake Dr., SW Lakewood, 98499
Phone (253) 584-4106 or (888) 858-4106
Website www.lakewoldgardens.org
Hours Apr.–Sept., Wednesday–Sunday, 10 a.m. to 4 p.m.; Oct.–Mar., Friday and Saturday, 10 a.m. to 4 p.m., Wednesdays in Aug., 10 a.m. to 8 p.m.
Fee Yes

Stroll through a period in garden history when classic European design came face to face with America's emerging landscape masters. Thomas D. Church, a leading landscape architect of the twentieth century, helped Eulalie Wagner make this garden her personal life project, which she left for all to enjoy. More than 900 rhododendrons grace the 10 acres.

Little & Lewis Water Gardens

Address 1940 Wing Point Way NE, Bainbridge Island, 98110
Phone (206) 842-8327
Website www.littleandlewis.com
Hours By appointment only
Fee Yes

The new home, studio, and garden of artists George Little and David Lewis, creators of unique concrete sculptures, opened in 2010. Examples of their beautiful, color-washed concrete sculpture are displayed. No appointment is needed on certain open gallery days throughout the summer.

W.W. Seymour Botanical Conservatory

Address 316 South G St., (in Wright Park), Tacoma, 98405
Phone (253) 591-5330
Website www.metroparkstacoma.org/page.php?id=21
Hours Tuesday–Sunday, 10 a.m. to 4:30 p.m.
Fee Donation requested

Voted the Best Place to Relax in Tacoma, the 100-year-old conservatory with its distinctive 12-sided central dome houses changing floral exhibits. More than 250 species provide color throughout the year, from azaleas and tulips to mums and paperwhite narcissus.

University of Washington Botanic Gardens

Address 3501 NE 41st St., Seattle, 98105
Phone (206) 543-8616
Website www.depts.washington.edu/uwbg
Hours Dusk to dawn, daily
Fee No

The Botanic Gardens was established in 2005 to unite the gardens and programs of the Washington Park Arboretum and the Center for Urban Horticulture. The nationally renowned living plant collection contains over 10,000 specimens. The Soest Display Garden recreates conditions found in the Pacific Northwest to evaluate plants.

University of Washington Medicinal Herb Garden

Address Stevens Way and Garfield Ln., Seattle, 98105
Phone (206) 543-0436
Website www.biology.washington.edu/mhg
Hours Daylight hours, daily
Fee No

At 2¹/₂ acres, this is one of the largest public gardens of its kind. It has 1,000 species from around the world used in historic and modern times for treating ailments, from colds to heart disease, as well as for food, fiber, dye, spices, and ceremonial purposes.

West Virginia Botanic Garden

Address 1061 Tyrone Rd., Morgantown, 26508
Phone (304) 376-2717
Website www.wvbg.org
Hours Daylight hours, daily
Fee No

The garden is being developed on 82 acres of the former Tibbs Run Reservoir, the ruins of which add historical interest to the property. There are cultivated flower beds at the entryway, in the Shade Garden, and in the Butterfly Garden. The remainder of the property is primitive and perfect for hiking, including a boardwalk through a wetland trail. It was the host institution for the 2011 International Master Gardener Conference.

C. Fred Edwards Conservatory

Address 2033 McCoy Rd., Huntington, 25701
Phone (304) 529-2701
Website www.hmoa.org/nature/conservatory
Hours Tuesday, 10 a.m. to 9 p.m., Wednesday–Saturday, 10 a.m. to 5 p.m., Sunday, noon to 5 p.m.
Fee Yes, free on Tuesdays

The conservatory is part of the Huntington Museum of Art and is West Virginia's only plant conservatory. It features tropical and subtropical plants, including 400 orchid varieties. Fragrance is also a key component in the conservatory with orange jessamine, stephanotis, and gingers.

Prabhupada's Palace Rose Garden

Address RD 1, NBU# 24 (Limestone Hill Palace Rd.), Moundsville, 26041
Phone (304) 843-1812
Website www.palaceofgold.com
Hours Apr.–Aug., 10 a.m. to 8 p.m.; Sept.–Mar., 10 a.m. to 5 p.m.
Fee Yes

Surrounding the Palace are two levels of terraces, replete with flower gardens, including large rose plantings, bordered by waterways with more than a hundred ornate fountains. From the terraces, the hills of West Virginia, Ohio, and Pennsylvania can be seen.

Boerner Botanical Garden

Address 9400 Boerner Dr., Hales Corners, 53130
Phone (414) 525-5650
Website www.boernerbotanicalgardens.org
Hours Late Apr.–early Oct., daily, 8 a.m. to sunset, other times
weather permitting; closed late Nov.–early Apr.
Fee Yes

Boerner Botanical Garden was named after one of Wisconsin's early landscape architects, who also designed the original five formal gardens. Today, a dozen gardens adorn Boerner, including ones for annuals, perennials, peonies, daylilies, roses, and herbs. It also encompasses a 1,000-acre arboretum. More than 900 perennials are labeled in the garden, and Master Gardeners have begun recording bloom cycles. In the Annual Garden, a low, decorative wall of native glacial stone outlines intensively planted display beds with sculpture and other art. The central water garden is a sea of water lilies.

Olbrich Botanical Gardens

Address 3330 Atwood Ave., Madison, 53704
Phone (608) 246-4550
Website www.olbrich.org
Hours Apr.–Sept., 8 a.m. to 8 p.m. daily; Oct., 9 a.m. to 6 p.m. daily;
Nov.–Mar., 9 a.m. to 4 p.m. Conservatory hours, Monday–
Saturday, 10 a.m. to 4 p.m., Sunday, 10 a.m. to 5 p.m.
Fee For conservatory; gardens free

In the outdoor gardens, the Thai Pavilion and Garden is the only one in the continental United States and the only one outside of Thailand surrounded by a garden. Olbrich's rose garden features innovative mixed borders of Midwest hardy shrub roses and perennials. You can stroll through other specialty gardens such as the Perennial Garden, Sunken Garden, and Herb Garden. The sunny Bolz Conservatory houses tropical plants, a rushing waterfall, free-flying birds, and blooming orchids.

Rotary Botanical Gardens

Address 1455 Palmer Dr., Janesville, 53545
Phone (608) 752-3885
Website www.rotarybotanicalgardens.org
Hours Apr. 15–Oct. 31, 8:30 a.m. to 6 p.m. daily;
Nov.–Dec., Monday–Friday, 8:30 a.m. to 4:30 p.m.,
Saturday and Sunday, 10 a.m. to 4 p.m.
Fee Yes

The 20-acre botanical garden is densely planted with more than 3,000 trees, shrubs, and vines; 2,000 perennials; 350,000 spring bulbs; and 75,000 annuals and other seasonal color. Themed gardens include French Formal Rose Garden; Italian, Japanese, English, and Cottage gardens; "Smelly," the Children's Garden; Sunken Garden; Gazebo Garden; and the American Garden Award garden. The last garden is a test site, one of 23, where visitors can rate the plants.

Allen Centennial Gardens

Address 620 Babcock Dr., Madison, 53706
Phone (608) 262-8406
Website www.allencentennialgardens.org
Hours Dawn to dusk, daily
Fee No

These gardens surround the home of four former deans of agriculture at the University of Wisconsin, and serve as educational and research resource for students and faculty. Annuals are planted in themes each year, and the Perennial Garden encompasses a mix of design styles and plants.

Green Bay Botanical Garden

Address 2600 Larsen Rd., Green Bay, 54303
Phone (920) 490-9457 or (877) 355-4224
Website www.gbbg.org
Hours Early June–Aug. 31, 9 a.m. to 8 p.m. daily; other times, year-round, vary
Fee Yes

Opened in 1996, the garden has 47 acres of about 20 natural, architectural, and cultivated areas, including a Children's Garden and an All-America Selections display garden. In 2010, the King Shade Garden opened. Thorne Fountain and Garden is a prime focal point.

Lynden Sculpture Garden

Address 2145 W. Brown Deer Rd., Milwaukee, 53217
Phone (414) 446-8794
Website www.lyndensculpturegarden.org
Hours Late May–early Sept., Monday, Tuesday, Friday, 10 a.m. to 5 p.m.,
Wednesday, 10 a.m. to 7:30 p.m., Saturday and Sunday, noon to 5 p.m.
Other hours vary by the season.
Fee Yes

This estate was opened to the public in 2009, which prompted a renovation of the house and gardens. The LEED-certified renovation used salvaged and reused materials and created sustainable gardens. Among the 50 sculptures on display are *Sinai* by Noguchi and *Argo* by Liberman.

Mitchell Park Conservatory

Address 524 South Layton Blvd., Milwaukee, 53215
Phone (414) 257-5611
Website www.county.milwaukee.gov/MitchellParkConserva10116.htm
Hours Monday–Friday, 9 a.m. to 5 p.m., Saturday and Sunday, 9 a.m. to 4 p.m.
Fee Yes

The original conservatory, built in 1898, was demolished in 1955. A local competition resulted in "the Domes," which opened in 1959 with three beehive-shaped domes 140 feet in diameter and 85 feet high. They hold collections of desert and tropical plants and seasonal flower shows.

Cheyenne Botanic Gardens

Address 710 S. Lions Park Dr., Cheyenne, 82001
Phone (307) 637-6458
Website www.botanic.org
Hours Grounds, dawn to dusk, Conservatory, Monday–Friday,
8 a.m. to 4 p.m., Saturday, 11 a.m. to 3:30 p.m.
Separate hours for Paul Smith Children's Village
Fee No

Highlights of the gardens are the Rotary Century Plazas, which depict plants from the 1700s, 1800s, and 1900s. The Rose Garden is planted with non-grafted hardy varieties. One garden is devoted to horticultural therapy. The Zigzag Walkway leads through the Discovery Pond Wetland Habitat. The Women's Civic League Peace Garden is a place of reflection, inspiration, and education. From April through November, the Perennial Border has something to offer. A 62-acre arboretum also is on the grounds.

Devonian Botanic Garden

Address Hwy. 60, Edmonton, AB, T6G 2E1
Phone (780) 987-3054
Website www.ales.ualberta.ca/devonian
Hours May 1–mid-Oct. daily, 10 a.m. to 5 p.m.;
May 23–Sept. 5, Monday–Wednesday, Friday–Sunday,
until 6 p.m., Thursday, until 8 p.m.
Fee Yes

The 190-acre University of Alberta Devonian Botanic Garden is minutes from the city and features 80 acres of display gardens and 110 additional acres of natural areas and ecological preserves. The indoor display features greenhouses and a butterfly house, outdoor displays include annuals and perennials; the Kurimoto Japanese Garden; rose, lilac, and peony collections; herb gardens; a native peoples' garden; extensive alpine gardens; and sensory and healing gardens. (Do not confuse this with Devonian Garden in downtown Calgary.)

Butchart Gardens

Address 800 Benvenuto Ave., Victoria, BC, V8M 1J8
Phone (866) 652-4422; (250) 652-4422
Website www.butchartgardens.com
Hours Open daily at 9 a.m., closing varies according to season
Fee Yes

Through successive generations of the Butchart family, one of the country's premier display gardens has retained much of its original design. It continues the Victorian tradition of seasonally changing its outstanding floral displays. The Rose Carousel is housed in the Children's Pavilion. During the summer, electric boats take visitors on a 45-minute tour of rugged shoreline and natural beauty of the Gowlland Tod Provincial Park. The ferry ride from Port Angeles, Washington, takes about 90 minutes.

Minter Gardens

Address 52893 Bunker Rd., Chilliwack, BC, V0X 1X1
Phone (888) 646-8377; (604) 794-7191
Website www.mintergardens.com
Hours Late Mar.–Apr., 10 a.m. to 5 p.m. daily;
May, 9 a.m. to 5:30 p.m.; June, 9 a.m. to 6 p.m.;
July and Aug., 9 a.m. to 7 p.m.; Sept., 9 a.m. to 5:30 p.m.;
Oct. 1–10, 10 a.m. to 5 p.m.
Fee Yes

More than 100,000 tulips adorn the gardens in spring as 1,000 rhodo-dendrons, planted amid cedar trees and rock wall terraces, provide color as spring turns to summer. Annuals take on the summer color duties, including topiaries and display beds pairing with the blooms in the Rose Garden. Woodlands and other features, including a curtain of water along a walkway, add drama. Minter's Country Garden Store is at 10015 Young Road North, not far from the gardens.

New Brunswick Botanical Garden

Address 15 Main St., Saint Jacques, NB, E7B 1A3
Phone (506) 737-4442
Website www.jardinnbgarden.com
Hours May, 9 a.m. to 5 p.m. daily; June, 9 a.m. to 6 p.m.;
July, 9 a.m. to 8 p.m.; Aug., 9 a.m. to 8 p.m.
Fee Yes

The New Brunswick Botanical Garden includes eight themed gardens and two arboretums on 20 acres along the banks of the magnificent Madawaska River. Enhance your sensory experience, with visits to the medicinal and aromatic plant garden, and see more than 100 species of therapeutic, cosmetic, and culinary plants. The herbalist's shop, resembling an apothecary, houses a kitchen for processing the herbs and demonstration dryers that exude subtle fragrances. The Visitor Center frequently has a butterfly exhibit.

Annapolis Royal Historic Gardens

Address 441 Saint George St., Annapolis Royal, NS, B0S 1A0
Phone (902) 532-7018
Website www.historicgardens.com
Hours Daily, hours vary by season
Fee Yes

On land that was settled in the seventeenth century, historical roots are what guide the development of the gardens as they tell the tale of Nova Scotia. The Innovative Garden demonstrates methods and plants that do well in urban settings and new introductions. The Rose Garden has about 230 roses, from the ancient Apothecary Rose through modern hybrids like the Canadian Explorer. The Victorian Garden, richly planted with annuals, reflects the prosperous days of shipbuilding and trade of the nineteenth century.

Niagara Parks Botanical Garden and School of Horticulture

Address 2565 N. Niagara Pkwy., Niagara Falls, ON, L2E 6T2
Phone (905) 356-8554; (877) 642-7275
Website www.niagaraparks.com
Hours Dawn to dusk, daily
Fee No

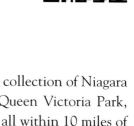

The gardens are part of the Niagara Garden Trail, a collection of Niagara Parks' owned and maintained gardens, including Queen Victoria Park, Oakes Garden Theatre, and the Floral Showhouse, all within 10 miles of the falls. There may be fees for some of these venues. Displays are changed for the seasons. A highlight is the famous 40-foot-diameter Floral Clock, which chimes on the quarter hour. The Fragrance Garden near the Greenhouse is a treat for the senses.

Royal Botanic Gardens

Address 680 Plains Rd. West, Burlington, ON, L7T 4H4
Phone (905) 527-1158; (800) 694-4769
Website www.rbg.ca
Hours 10 a.m. to 8 p.m. daily
Fee Yes

At 2,700 acres, this is the largest botanical garden in North America and one of the most complete. The first garden built in 1929 is the rock garden, which is now famous for its large displays of annuals. Hendrie Park is the center of the floral displays, a fine collection of fragrant flowers, water gardens, medicinal gardens, and two acres of roses of all types. The Royal Botanical Gardens Centre is near the arboretum and houses indoor and outdoor displays, including the Mediterranean Garden.

Spadina Historic House and Gardens

Address 285 Spadina Rd., Toronto, ON, M5R 2V5
Phone (416) 392-6910
Website www.toronto.ca/culture/museums/spadina.htm
Hours Jan.–Mar., Saturday–Sunday, noon–5 p.m.;
Apr.–Labor Day, Tuesday–Sunday, noon to 5 pm.;
Sept.–Jan., Saturday–Sunday, noon–5 pm., Tuesday–Friday, noon to 4 p .m.
Fee Yes, for house, gardens free

Four generations of the Austin family occupied this house for more than 100 years. Volunteers from Toronto's garden clubs and history buffs restored the house and elaborate gardens to their former splendor. The formal flower beds have been recreated using archival photographs, drawings, and family letters and stories. Original plants of the 300 varieties showcased include historic oaks, peonies, lilacs, daylilies, and irises. The bedding plants change seasonally.

Jardins des Floralies

Address 1 Circuit Gilles-Villeneuve, Montreal, QB, H3C 1A9
Phone (514) 872-6120
Website www.parcjeandrapeau.com
Hours 7 a.m. to 9 p.m. daily
Fee Yes, for parking

The gardens are the legacy of the Floralies International, an international horticultural fair held in a different city every 10 years. They are located in a park on Ile Notre-Dame and Ile Sainte-Helene islands in the St. Lawrence River.

Muttart Conservatory

Address 9626-96A St., Edmonton, AB, T6C 4L8

Phone (780) 496-8755

Website www.edmonton.ca/attractions_recreation/attractions/muttart-conservatory.aspx

Hours Weekdays, 10 a.m. to 5 p.m.; weekends and holidays, 11 a.m. to 5 p.m.

Fee Yes, occasional free admission days

Known as the "Pyramids," the conservatory is home to art exhibits as well as arid, temperate, and tropical plants. A waterfall cascades into the center where small fish and water lilies make their home. Some of the plants in the Orchid Hut Houses perfume the air.

Glendale Gardens at the Horticulture Centre of the Pacific

Address 505 Quayle Rd., Victoria, BC, V9E 2J7

Phone (250) 479-6162

Website www.hcp.ca

Hours May 1–Sept. 30, Monday–Friday, 8 a.m. to 6 p.m., Saturday and Sunday, 9 a.m. to 4 p.m.; Oct. 1–Apr. 30, daily, 9 a.m. to 4 p.m.

Fee Yes

Known by many as Glendale Gardens, the 9 acres of spectacular demonstration gardens showcase over 10,000 varieties of plants labeled and displayed growing in their ideal conditions. There's a Zen Garden, Winter Garden, Dry Garden, and Hardy Fuchsia Garden. The 93-acre Conservation Park is free.

University of British Columbia Botanic Garden

Address 1895 SW Marine Dr., Vancouver, BC, V6P 6B2

Phone (604) 822-3928

Website www.botanicalgarden.ubc.ca

Hours Weekdays, 9 a.m. to 5 p.m.; Weekends, 9:30 a.m. to 5 p.m.

Fee No

Gardens include a Carolinian Forest, Physic Garden, Alpine Garden, Food, Garden, British Columbian Rain Forest, and Asian Garden. Not far from here is Nitobe Memorial Garden, where each tree, stone, and shrub has been deliberately placed to reflect an idealized conception and symbolic representation of nature.

Living Prairie Museum

Address 2795 Ness Ave., Winnipeg, MB, R3J 3S4

Phone (204) 832-0167

Website www.winnipeg.ca/publicworks/naturalist/livingprairie

Hours Museum, May and June, Sunday, 10 a.m. to 5 p.m.; July–Aug., daily, 10 a.m. to 5 p.m.; prairie, daily, dawn to dusk

Fee No

The museum and preserve demonstrate a tall grass prairie with more than 160 plant species. Tall grass prairies grew through North America from Manitoba to Texas, but now only small remnants remain. One of the largest undisturbed areas was found in a residential neighborhood in Winnipeg.

Horticultural Gardens Rockwood Park

Address 48 Seely St., Saint John, NB, E2K 4B2
    Phone (506) 657-1773
Website www.rockwoodparkcampground.com/horticulturalSociety.html
    Hours Daily
      Fee No

The Saint John Horticultural Association was formed in 1893 to design gardens around Rockwood Park Campground. Today, the park has more than 2,200 acres and the society maintains the public display gardens and greenhouses.

Newfoundland Memorial University Botanical Garden

Address 306 Mount Scio Rd., St. John's, NL, A1B 4L6
    Phone (709) 864-8596
Website www.mun.ca/botgarden
    Hours May 1–Sept. 30, 10 a.m. to 5 p.m. daily; Oct. 1–Nov. 30, daily, 10 a.m. to 4 p.m.;
                Dec. 1–Apr. 30, daily, 8:30 a.m. to 4 p.m.
      Fee Yes

The theme gardens include the cottage garden, rock gardens (including a limestone rockery and scree), alpine house, peat and woodland beds, Newfoundland heritage garden, rhododendron dell, wildlife garden, shade garden, medicinal garden, dried flower garden, vegetable garden, and compost demonstration garden.

Halifax Public Garden

Address 5665 Spring Garden Rd., Halifax, NS, B3J 2L1
 Phone (902) 490-3995
Website www.halifaxpublicgardens.ca
 Hours Spring–fall, 8 a.m. to dusk, daily
 Fee Free

The ornate gates lead visitors to this rare example of an intact formal Victorian public garden, which opened in 1867. As with gardens of this type, beds are planted along pathways or hidden by curves in the sidewalk. Flora, Ceres, Diana, and other statues adorn the gardens.

Guild Inn Sculpture Garden

Address 201 Guildwood Pkwy., Scarborough, ON, M1E 1K7
 Phone (416) 397-2628
Website www.toronto.ca/culture/the_guild.htm
 Hours Daily
 Fee No

The gardens represent a personal building conservation program. Fragments from demolished buildings around the area were rescued and re-erected as a sculpture garden, including Corinthian columns from the Bank of Toronto. The garden serves as a venue for musical concerts and other performances.

Shakespearean Gardens

Address Huron St. (Hwy. 8) and York St., Stratford, ON, N5A 5S4
Phone (519) 271-0250
Website www.city.stratford.on.ca/site_ourcitylife/know_your_city_
garden_and_natural_areas.asp
Hours Daily
Fee No

This Shakespeare Garden exemplifies an Elizabethan garden, including perennials, herbs, and other plants that had roles in the bard's poems and plays. With recent renovations, it is closer to the original 1926 design. The local horticultural society offers tours through many of the gardens in Stratford.

Toronto Music Garden

Address 475 Queen's Quay West, Toronto, ON, M5J 2G8
Phone (416) 973-4000
Website www.toronto.ca/parks/featured-parks/music-garden
Hours Dawn to dusk, daily
Fee No

The garden was inspired by Bach and is designed in the spirit of music, dance, and artistic genius. The public space, which opened in 1990, has regular concerts and other performances. It is a symbol of Toronto's participation in the international community and is a place for everyone to enjoy.

CANADA

Montreal Botanical Garden and Insectarium

Address 4101 rue Sherbrooke Est, Montreal, QB, H1X 2B2
Phone (514) 872-1400
Website www2.ville.montreal.qc.ca/jardin/en/menu.htm
Hours 9 a.m. to 6 p.m. daily
Fee Yes

The Insectarium underwent a facelift and reopened in 2011. It is the largest insectarium in North America and features dead and live bugs, many of which can be touched by visitors. The Botanical Garden is one of the largest in the world with more than 22,000 species. It has a Japanese and Chinese garden and dozens of others, including First Nations Garden, Lilac Collection, Toxic Plant Garden, the Leslie-Hancock Secret Garden, and a Tree House.

Wascana Centre

Address 2900 Wascana Dr., Regina, SK, S4P 4K6
Phone (306) 522-3661
Website www.wascana.sk.ca
Hours Daily
Fee No

This 2300-acre urban park encompasses many important buildings in Regina, combining land with government cultural and recreational facilities. The secluded Lady Slipper Courtyard is named for the native orchid.

Garden Walks, Garden Talks & Garden Events

ALABAMA

ALDRIDGE GARDENS www.aldridgegardens.com
Art in the Gardens—The Art Show for Alabama Artists, first weekend in June

BELLINGRATH GARDENS AND HOME www.bellingrath.org
Festival of Flowers, March–April
Magic Christmas in Lights, Friday after Thanksgiving through December

BIRMINGHAM BOTANICAL GARDEN www.bbgardens.org
Glorious Gardens, Spring
Spring Plant Sale, mid-April
Antiques at the Gardens, October

HUNTSVILLE BOTANICAL GARDEN www.hsvbg.org
Spring Festival of Flowers, April
Plant Sale, mid-April
Scarecrow Trail, September and October
Galaxy of Lights, mid-November through December

MOBILE BOTANICAL GARDEN www.mobilebotanicalgardens.org
Gallery of Garden, mid-May
Plant Sales, mid- to late-October
Festival of Flowers www.festivalofflowers.com, March–April

ALASKA

ALASKA BOTANICAL GARDEN www.alaskabg.org
Garden Fair & Garden Art Show, June

ARIZONA

ARBORETUM AT FLAGSTAFF www.thearb.org
Plant Sale, July
Fall Open House, October

DESERT BOTANICAL GARDEN www.dbg.org
Music in the Garden, Fridays
Los Noches de las Luminarias December

TUCSON BOTANICAL GARDENS www.tucsonbotanical.org
Twilight Third Thursday, Visual and Performing Arts, Summer

ARKANSAS

BOTANICAL GARDEN OF THE OZARKS www.bgozarks.org
Firefly Fling: The Summer Festival for Families, July

GARVAN WOODLAND GARDENS www.garvangardens.com
Holiday Lights Display, Thanksgiving—December 31

ARKANSAS FLOWER AND GARDEN SHOW www.arflowerandgardenshow.org, March

CALIFORNIA

ANZA-BORREGO ANNUAL DESERT GARDEN TOUR www.abdnha.org, March

CALIFORNIA NATIVE PLANT TOUR www.californianativegardentour.org, June

CALIFORNIA STATE FLOWER, FOOD & GARDEN SHOW www.calstategardenshow.com, April

ENCINITAS GARDEN FESTIVAL & TOUR www.encinitasgardenfestival.org, late April

LOS ANGELES HOME & GARDEN SHOW www.lagardenshow.com, late April

MISSION HILL GARDEN WALK www.missionhillsgardenclub.org, May

NORTHERN CALIFORNIA HOME & LANDSCAPE SHOW www.homeandlandscapeexpo.com, Jan.

SACRAMENTO HOME & GARDEN SHOW www.sachomeandgardenshow.com, March

SAN FRANCISCO FLOWER & GARDEN SHOW www.sfgardenshow.com, March

SOUTHERN CALIFORNIA SPRING GARDEN SHOW www.springgardenshow.com, late April

VENICE HOME AND GARDEN TOUR vwww.venicegardentour.org, May

COLORADO

DENVER BOTANICAL GARDEN www.botanicgardens.org
Popular music concerts throughout the summer; Ghost tours in October

CONNECTICUT

CONNECTICUT FLOWER GARDEN SHOW www.ctflowershow.com, late February

DELAWARE

DELAWARE CENTER FOR HORTICULTURE, RARE PLANT AUCTION www.thedch.org, April

UNIVERSITY OF DELAWARE BOTANIC GARDENS ag.udel.edu/udbg/events/annualsale.html
Spring and Fall Plant Sales, April and September

DISTRICT OF COLUMBIA

WASHINGTON HOME & GARDEN SHOW www.washingtonhomeandgardenshow.com, March

FLORIDA

ALBIN POLASEK MUSEUM & SCULPTURE GARDENS www.polasek.org/wppo
Winter Park Paint Out, April

CENTRAL FLORIDA HOME & GARDEN SHOW www.centralflhomeandgardenshow.com,
April, Orlando

FAIRCHILD TROPICAL BOTANIC GARDEN MANGO FESTIVAL www.fairchildgarden.org, July

KANAPAHA BOTANICAL GARDENS www.kanapaha.org/spring.htm, March

GEORGIA

SOUTHEASTERN FLOWER SHOW www.sehort.org, February, Atlanta

SAVANNAH TOUR OF HOMES & GARDENS www.savannahtourofhomes.org, March

HAWAII

BIG ISLAND ASSOCIATION OF NURSERYMEN PLANT SALE www.hawaiiplants.com, early March

IDAHO

SAWTOOTH BOTANICAL GARDEN, GARDEN DAY www.sbgarden.org, July

ILLINOIS

CHICAGO BOTANIC GARDEN, A BLOOMIN' FESTIVAL www.chicagobotanic.org/bloomin/index.php, mid-May

CHICAGO FLOWER & GARDEN SHOW www.chicagoflower.com, March

HYDE PARK GARDEN FAIR SPRING SALE http://www.hydeparkgardenfair.org, mid-May, Chicago

ILLINOIS SYMPHONY ORCHESTRA GUILD SPRING GARDEN TOUR www.ilsymphony.org, June, Springfield

SHEFFIELD GARDEN WALK www.sheffieldfestivals.org, July, Chicago

INDIANA

ANNUAL QUILT GARDENS ALONG THE HERITAGE TRAIL, late May through early October, Elkhart

FORT WAYNE HOME AND GARDEN SHOW www.premierhomeshows.com, March

GARFIELD PARK CONSERVATORY & SUNKEN GARDEN www.garfieldgardensconservatory.org **Conservatory Crossing Holiday Train Exhibit,** Thanksgiving–December

INDIANA FLOWER & PATIO SHOW www.indianaflowerandpatioshow.com, March, Indianapolis

INDIANA NATIVE PLANT & WILDFLOWER SOCIETY NATIVE PLANT TOUR www.inpaws.org, July

INDIANAPOLIS MUSEUM OF ART PERENNIAL PREMIER www.imamuseum.org/special-event/perennial-premiere, mid-April

ORCHARD IN BLOOM www.orchardinbloom.org, late April, Indianapolis

IOWA

REIMAN GARDENS ART FAIR www.reimangardens.iastate.edu, July

SEED SAVERS EXCHANGE www.seedsavers.org **Annual Conference and Campout,** mid-July

KANSAS

KANSAS GARDEN SHOW www.ksexpo.com, mid-February, Topeka

KENTUCKY

CENTRAL KENTUCKY HOME, GARDEN & FLOWER SHOW www.ckyhomeshow.com, April, Lexington

HEART OF KENTUCKY FARM, HOME & GARDEN SHOW www.visitlebanonky.com/farmhomegardenshow.html, April, Lebanon

OLD LOUISVILLE GARDEN TOUR www.oldlouisvillegardentour.com, July

LOUISIANA

SOUTHWEST LOUISIANA GARDEN SHOW www.gardenfest.org, March, Lake Charles

SECRET GARDENS TOUR www.secretgardenstour.org, March, New Orleans

MAINE

COASTAL MAINE BOTANICAL GARDENS, MIDSUMMER EVENT www.mainegardens.org, July, Boothbay

MARYLAND

MARYLAND HOME & GARDEN SHOW www.mdhomeandgarden.com/spring, March, Timonium

MARYLAND HOUSE & GARDEN PILGRIMAGE www.mhgp.org, May, Baltimore

MASSACHUSETTS

HIDDEN GARDENS OF BEACON HILL www.beaconhillgardenclub.org/tour.html, May

BOSTON FLOWER & GARDEN SHOW www.masshort.org/Blooms-and-the-Boston-Flower-&-Garden-Show, March

FLOWER & PATIO SHOW/OUTDOOR LIVING EXPO centralmaflowershow.com, March, Worcester

MICHIGAN

LOCAL MOTION GREEN GARDEN TOUR www.localmotiongreen.org, June, Grosse Pointe

EAST MICHIGAN HOME & GARDEN SHOW www.eventsinamerica.com, March, Pontiac

WEST MICHIGAN HOME & GARDEN SHOW www.eventsinamerica.com, March, Grand Rapids

MINNESOTA

MINNEAPOLIS HOME & GARDEN SHOW www.homeandgardenshow.com, February–March, Minneapolis

MINNESOTA STATE HORTICULTURAL SOCIETY SPRING OPEN HOUSE www.northerngardener.org, June, Roseville

MISSISSIPPI

HOME & GARDEN SHOW www.gulfcoast.org/events/index.cfm?EventID=529, late March–early April, Biloxi

MISSOURI

METROPOLITAN LAWN AND GARDEN SHOW www.patrihaproductions.com, February, Kansas City

MISSOURI BOTANICAL GARDEN ORCHID SHOW, February–March, St. Louis

GARDENLAND EXPRESS ANNUAL HOLIDAY FLOWER AND TRAIN SHOW www.mobot.org, November–January

ST. LOUIS HOME & GARDEN SHOW www.stlhomeshow.com/homegarden, February

MONTANA

GREAT FALLS HOME AND GARDEN SHOW www.greatfallscvb.visitmt.com/categories/moreinfo.asp?IDRRecordID=9799&siteid=26, February

TIZER BOTANIC GARDENS & ARBORETUM, FAIRY & WIZARDS FESTIVAL www.tizergardens.com, July

NEBRASKA

HOME & GARDEN EXPO AND LAWN FLOWER & PATIO SHOW www.nahb.cc, Norfolk

OMAHA HOME & GARDEN SHOW www.showofficeonline.com/2009HomeGardenExpoInfo.htm, February

NEVADA

RENO SPRING HOME & GARDEN SHOW www.lockettshows.com/spring-home-show.htm, March

NEW HAMPSHIRE

STRAWBERY BANKE, NEW HAMPSHIRE FALL FESTIVAL www.strawberybanke.org, early October

NEW JERSEY

GARDEN CLUB OF FAIR HAVEN GARDEN TOUR AND PLANT SALE njclubs.esiteasp.com/gardencluboffairhaven/tourandplantsale.nxg, May

NEW JERSEY FLOWER & GARDEN SHOW www.macevents.com/show.cfm/eventID/121, Edison, February

NEW JERSEY HOME & GARDEN SHOW http://www.newjerseyhomeandgardenshow.com/, March, Atlantic City

SPRINGFEST FLOWER & GARDEN SHOW www.njstatefair.org/springfest/springfest.cfm, March, Augusta

RUTGERS GARDENS, SPRING FLOWER FAIR www.rutgersgardens.rutgers.edu, early May

NEW MEXICO

ALBUQUERQUE BOTANIC GARDEN www.cabq.gov/biopark/garden
River of Lights Holiday Display, December

ALBUQUERQUE HOME & GARDEN SHOW abqhomeandgardenshow.com, April

SANTA FE BOTANICAL GARDEN www.santafebotanicalgarden.org
Garden Tours of Santa Fe, June

NEW YORK

BROOKLYN BOTANIC GARDEN www.bbg.org
   Sakura Matsuri Cherry Blossom Festival, late April

CNY BLOOMS FLOWER & GARDEN SHOW www.cnyblooms.com, early March, Syracuse

GARDENSCAPE ROCHESTER FLOWER SHOW www.rochesterflowershow.com, March

GARDEN WALK BUFFALO www.gardenwalkbuffalo.com, late July

PLANTASIA Hamburg www.plantasiany.com/index.html, March

NORTH CAROLINA

CAPE FEAR GARDEN CLUB AZALEA GARDEN TOUR www.ncazaleafestival.org, April

NORTH CAROLINA BOTANICAL GARDEN ncbg.unc.edu/pages/29/#sculpture
   Annual Sculpture in the Garden, late-September to early October

SOUTHERN SPRING HOME & GARDEN SHOW www.southernshows.com, February–March, Raleigh

WING HAVEN SPRING PLANT SALE www.winghavengardens.com, April, Charlotte
   Fall Plant Sale, October

NORTH DAKOTA

DAKOTA GARDEN EXPO www.dakotagardener.com/expo, May, Bismarck

OHIO

BARBERTON MUM FEST www.cityofbarberton.com/govt/MumFest, late September

CINCINNATI FLOWER SHOW Cincinnati www.cincyflowershow.com, April

CINCINNATI HOME & GARDEN SHOW www.hartproductions.com/home-and-garden-show, February–March

CLEVELAND HOME & GARDEN SHOW www.homeandflower.com/cleveland, January, Euclid

GERMAN VILLAGE HAUS UND GARTEN TOUR www.germanvillage.com, late June, Columbus

TOLEDO BOTANICAL GARDEN www.toledogarden.org
   Crosby Festival of the Arts, late June

WASSO GARDEN TOUR www.springfieldsym.org/gardentour.html, Springfield, July

OKLAHOMA

OKLAHOMA CITY HOMES AND GARDEN SHOW www.oklahomacityhomeshow.com, January

TULSA HOME & GARDEN SHOW www.tulsahba.com, March

OREGON

POLK COUNTY HOME & GARDEN SHOW www.polkhomeandgardenshow.com, February, Rickreall

PORTLAND HOME & GARDEN SHOW www.otshows.com/phs, February

PORTLAND FALL HOME & GARDEN SHOW www.otshows.com/pfhs,
late September—early October

PORTLAND YARD, GARDEN & PATIO SHOW ygpshow.com, February

PENNSYLVANIA

HOME & GARDEN SHOW pghhome.com/index.php , March, Pittsburgh

PENNSYLVANIA GARDEN EXPO www.jpiexpo.com/pagardenexpo, February, Harrisburg

PHILADELPHIA INTERNATIONAL FLOWER SHOW www.theflowershow.com, March

RHODE ISLAND

RHODE ISLAND SPRING FLOWER & GARDEN SHOW www.flowershow.com, February, Providence

SOUTH CAROLINA

FESTIVAL OF HOUSES AND GARDENS www.historiccharleston.org, mid-March to mid-April,
Charleston

SOUTH DAKOTA

ALICE SMITH FLOWER SHOW www.travelsd.com/Events/Details?id=75935, July, Hill City

TENNESSEE

ANTIQUES AND GARDEN SHOW www.antiquesandgardenshow.com, February, Nashville

BLOOM 'N' GARDEN EXPO LAWN & GARDEN SHOW www.bloomngarden.com, April, Franklin

CHEEKWOOD BOTANICAL GARDEN FAMILY NIGHT OUT www.cheekwood.org, June–July, Nashville

NASHVILLE LAWN & GARDEN SHOW www.nashvillelawnandgardenshow.com, March

TEXAS

AUSTIN FALL HOME & GARDEN SHOW www.austinhomeandgardenshow.com, late August

FORT WORTH HOME & GARDEN SHOW www.texashomeandgarden.com , August

DALLAS HOME & GARDEN SHOW www.texashomeandgarden.com, September

TEXAS HOME & GARDEN SHOW www.texashomeandgarden.com, September, Houston

TEXAS ROSE FESTIVAL www.texasrosefestival.com, mid-October, Tyler

UTAH

UTAH VALLEY SPRING HOME EXPO www.uvexpo.com/home_garden, April, Orem

VERMONT

VERMONT FLOWER SHOW greenworksvermont.org/vermont-flower-show, March, North Ferrisburgh

VERMONT HOME & FLOWER SHOW www.vthomeandgardenshow.com, mid-April, Essex Junction

VIRGINIA

DOMINION GARDENFEST OF LIGHTS www.lewisginter.org, Thanksgiving to early January, Richmond

HISTORIC GARDEN WEEK www.vagardenweek.org, April, state-wide

MAYMONT FLOWER & GARDEN SHOW www.macevents.com/show.cfm/eventID/139, February, Richmond

VIRGINIA FLOWER & GARDEN SHOW www.vahort.org, early March, Virginia Beach

VIRGINIA HOME & GARDEN SHOW www.agievents.com/shows/display.cfm?show ID=41&showtypeid=4&src=22, January, Doswell

WASHINGTON

NORTHWEST FLOWER & GARDEN SHOW www.gardenshow.com, February

TACOMA HOME & GARDEN SHOW www.otshows.com/ths, January

WEST VIRGINIA

HOME & GARDEN SHOW www.wsaz.com/wsazevents/headlines/2580746.html, March, Huntington

WEST VIRGINIA HOME, GARDEN AND FARM SHOW wboy.com/story.cfm?func=viewstory& storyid=96273, mid-March, Morgantown

WISCONSIN

GARDEN EXPO www.wigardenexpo.com, February, Madison

HOME & GARDEN SHOW www.realtorshomeandgardenshow.com, March–April, Milwaukee

WBAY HOME & GARDEN SHOW www.wbay.com/story/35056/wbay-home-and-garden-show, March, Green Bay

WYOMING

CHEYENNE HOME & GARDEN SHOW www.wyomingtourism.org/overview/Cheyenne-Home-and-Garden-Show/747439, March

CANADA

CANADA BLOOMS www.canadablooms.com, March, Toronto

Major Garden Events and Tours of England, Europe, and Other Parts of the World

GARDEN EVENTS

CHELSEA FLOWER SHOW www.chs.org.uk/Shows-Events/RHS.Chelsea-Flower-Show
 London Forum, May

The Chelsea Flower Show has been the one of the world's leading horticultural event since the first show in 1913 when gardeners from the large private estates created brilliant displays. Today, you will be see an international collection of magnificent blooms and specimen trees alongside an incredible range of exhibition gardens. This unique event is lovingly prepared by the country's leading horticulturists transforming several acres into an extraordinary vista of gardens.

FLORIADE—WORLD HORTICULTURAL EXPO www.floriade.com
 The Netherlands, April–October

Floriade promises to be an event where you'll learn about nature and find out just how important flowers, plants, trees, vegetables and fruit are in our daily lives. Designed specially for this event, the ultra-sustainable Villa Flora is home to the one of the biggest indoor flower shows. You can also find out how nature and industry actually complement each other and how horticulture can be used as a major economic engine.

GARDEN TOURS

ADDERLEY TRAVEL www.adderleytravel.com
 Cornwall & Bath, April
 The Bluebell Tour, April–May, Sussex
 Highland & Islands, May
 Chelsea Flower Show, May

AP TOURING www.aptouring.com
 French and Italian Gardens in Spring, May, Paris to Rome
 Chelsea Flower Show, May, UK and Wales Gardens
 Italian Lakes and Croatian Wildflowers, May–June
 UK Gardens and Hampton Court Flower Show, June–July

BRIGHTWATER HOLIDAYS www.brightwaterholidays.com
 Ecuador: Orchids and Incas, January
 Galicia's Camellia Route, November
 The Gardens of Japan, November, Japan

COOPERSMITH'S GARDEN TOURS www.coopersmiths.com
- **Belgium, Holland, & the Floriade,** May
- **West Country Gardens & Stately Homes,** June
- **Italian & French Rivieras,** September
- **Springtime in the Cotswolds,** May
- **Gardens & Castles of Wales + Chelsea,** May
- **Durham & Northumberland,** June–July

GARDENING TOURS www.gardeningtours.com
- **Northern India Garden Tour,** March
- **Floriade/Keukenhof,** April
- **Morocco,** May
- **Chelsea Flower Show Tour,** May
- **Italy,** June
- **South Africa,** October

LYNOTT TOURS www.lynotttours.com/b-gardens.htm
- **Chelsea Flower Show Tour,** May
- **Ireland & Britain Garden Tour,** May–June
- **Cotswolds English Garden Tours,** May–July

We are sure you know of other tours and companies that warrant inclusion. Drop us a note at Cool Springs Press if you know of another great garden tour.

State & Regional Maps

Check out the maps on the following pages as you are planning your trip. Each state or regional map pinpoints the location of each of the gardens in this book so you will have a sense of its location and other gardens in its proximity. If you have a GPS system on your smartphone, you can even link to GPS to determine specific driving directions and distances. And remember—the QR code on page 13 links to the listing of all the gardens.

Note: Maps are not to scale.

ALASKA

2

1

3

ALASKA (3)

1. **Alaska Botanical Garden, Anchorage**
2. University of Alaska Fairbanks Georgeson Botanical Garden, Fairbanks
3. Jensen-Olson Arboretum, Juneau

1

2
3

HAWAII (3)

1. **Na 'Aina Kai Botanical Gardens, Sculpture Park & Hardwood Plantation, Kilauea**
2. Honolulu Botanical Gardens, Honolulu
3. University of Hawaii Lyon Arboretum and Botanical Garden, Honolulu

HAWAII

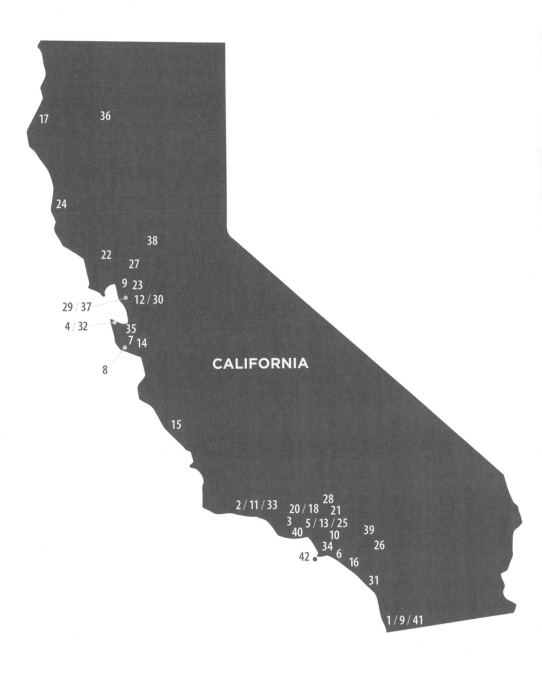

17

36

24

38

22

27

9 23

12 / 30

29 / 37

4 / 32

35

7 14

8

CALIFORNIA

15

2 / 11 / 33

28

20 / 18

21

3

5 / 13 / 25

40

10

39

34

6

26

42

16

31

1 / 9 / 41

CALIFORNIA (42)

1. **Balboa Park Garden, San Diego**
2. Casa del Herrero, Santa Barbara
3. Conejo Valley Botanic Garden, Thousand Oaks
4. Conservatory of Flowers, San Francisco
5. Descanso Gardens, La Cañada Flintridge
6. Earl Burns Miller Japanese Garden California State University at Long Beach, Long Beach
7. Elizabeth Gamble Garden, Palo Alto
8. **Filoli Garden, Woodside**
9. Forrest Deanery Native Plant Botanic Garden, Benicia
10. Fullerton Arboretum, Fullerton
11. **Ganna Walska Lotusland Garden, Santa Barbara**
12. Gardens at Heather Farm, Walnut Creek
13. Getty Center, Los Angeles
14. Hakone Gardens, Saratoga
15. **Hearst Castle Gardens, San Simeon**
16. Hortense Miller Garden, Laguna Beach
17. Humboldt Botanical Garden, Eureka
18. **Huntington Botanical Gardens, San Marino**
19. Japanese Friendship Garden, San Diego
20. The Japanese Garden, Van Nuys
21. **Los Angeles County Arboretum & Botanical Garden, Arcadia**
22. Luther Burbank Home and Gardens, Santa Rosa
23. Markham Nature Park and Arboretum, Concord
24. Mendocino Coast Botanical Gardens, Fort Bragg
25. Mildred E. Mathias Garden at UCLA, Los Angeles
26. Moorten Botanical Gardens, Palm Springs
27. Quarryhill Botanical Garden, Glen Ellen
28. **Rancho Santa Ana Botanic Garden, Claremont**
29. Regional Parks Botanic Garden, Berkeley
30. Ruth Bancroft Garden, Walnut Creek
31. **San Diego Botanic Garden, Encinitas**
32. **San Francisco Botanical Garden at Strybing Arboretum, San Francisco**
33. Santa Barbara Botanical Garden, Santa Barbara
34. South Coast Botanic Garden, Palos Verdes Peninsula
35. Sunset Garden, Menlo Park
36. Turtle Bay Exploration Park's McConnell Arboretum and Botanical Gardens, Redding
37. **University of California Berkeley Botanical Garden, Berkeley**
38. University of California, Davis Arboretum, Davis
39. University of California, Riverside Botanic Gardens, Riverside
40. Virginia Robinson Gardens, Beverly Hills
41. Water Conservation Garden, El Cajon
42. Wrigley Memorial Botanic Garden on Catalina Island, Avalon

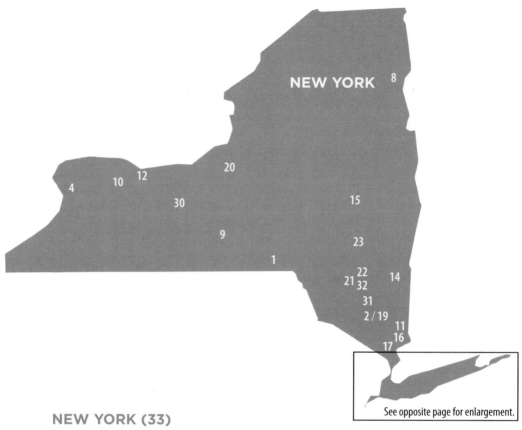

NEW YORK (33)

1. Binghamton Zoo at Ross Park, Binghamton
2. Boscobel House and Gardens, Garrison
3. **Brooklyn Botanic Garden, Brooklyn**
4. **Buffalo and Erie County Botanical Gardens, Buffalo**
5. **Central Park Conservatory Garden, New York City**
6. Clark Botanic Garden, Albertson
7. **Cloisters Museum & Gardens, New York City**
8. Colonial Garden, Elizabethtown
9. Cornell Plantations, Ithaca
10. Genesee County Village & Museum, Mumford
11. Hammond Museum and Japanese Stroll Garden, North Salem
12. Highland Botanical Garden and Lamberton Conservatory, Rochester
13. John P. Humes Japanese Stroll Garden, Mill Neck
14. Innisfree Garden, Millbrook
15. Landis Arboretum, Esperance
16. Lasdon Park, Arboretum and Veterans Memorial, Katonah
17. Lyndhurst, Tarrytown

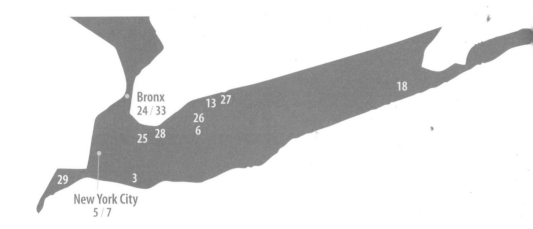

18. Madoo Conservancy, Sagaponack
19. Manitoga/The Russel Wright Design Center, Garrison
20. E.M. Mills Memorial Rose Garden, Syracuse
21. **Mohonk Preserve, Gardiner**
22. Montgomery Place, Annandale-on-Hudson
23. Mountain Top Arboretum, Tannersville
24. **New York Botanical Garden, Bronx**
25. **Noguchi Museum and Sculpture Garden, Long Island City**
26. Old Westbury Gardens, Old Westbury
27. **Planting Fields Arboretum, Oyster Bay**
28. **Queens Botanical Garden, Flushing**
29. Snug Harbor Cultural Center & Botanical Garden, Staten Island
30. Sonnenberg Gardens & Mansion State Historic Park, Canandaigua
31. Stonecrop Gardens, Cold Spring
32. **Vanderbilt Mansion Gardens, Hyde Park**
33. **Wave Hill, Bronx**

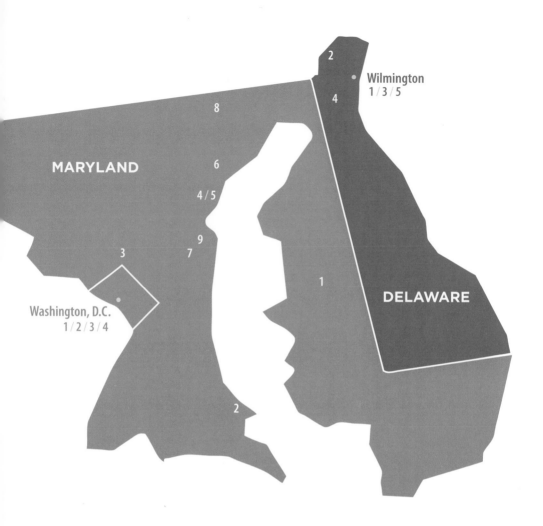

DELAWARE (5)

1. **Delaware Center for Horticulture, Wilmington**
2. Mt. Cuba Center, Hockessin
3. Nemours Mansion & Gardens, Wilmington
4. University of Delaware Botanic Gardens, Newark
5. Winterthur Museum, Garden & Library, Wilmington

WASHINGTON, DC (4)

1. Dumbarton Oaks
2. **Hillwood Estate, Museum & Gardens**
3. **United States Botanic Garden**
4. U.S. National Arboretum

MARYLAND (9)

1. Adkins Arboretum, Ridgely
2. Annmarie Sculpture Gardens, Solomons
3. **Brookside Gardens, Wheaton**
4. Cylburn Garden Center, Baltimore
5. **Druid Hill Park Conservatory, Baltimore**
6. Hampton National Historic Site, Towson
7. Historic London Town and Gardens, Edgewater
8. Ladew Topiary Garden, Monkton
9. **William Paca Gardens, Annapolis**

NEW JERSEY (22)

1. Camden Children's Garden, Camden
2. Colonial Park Aboretum and Gardens, Somerset
3. Cross Estate Gardens, Bernardsville
4. Frelinghuysen Arboretum, Morris Township
5. **Garden for the Blind and Physically Handicapped, Iselin**
6. Greenwood Gardens, Short Hills
7. **Grounds For Sculpture, Hamilton**
8. James Rose Center, Ridgewood
9. Laurelwood Arboretum, Wayne
10. **Leamings Run Gardens, North Cape May Court House**
11. Leonard Buck Garden, Far Hills
12. Macculloch Hall Historical Museum and Gardens, Morristown
13. New Jersey Botanical Garden, Ringwood
14. **Presby Memorial Iris Gardens, Upper Montclair**
15. Prospect House & Garden, Princeton
16. Reeves-Reed Arboretum, Summit
17. **Rutgers Gardens, New Brunswick**
18. Sister Mary Grace Burns Arboretum, Lakewood
19. **Van Vleck House & Gardens, Montclair**
20. Well-Sweep Herb Farm, Port Murray
21. Wick House Herb Garden, Morristown
22. Willowwood Arboretum, Chester

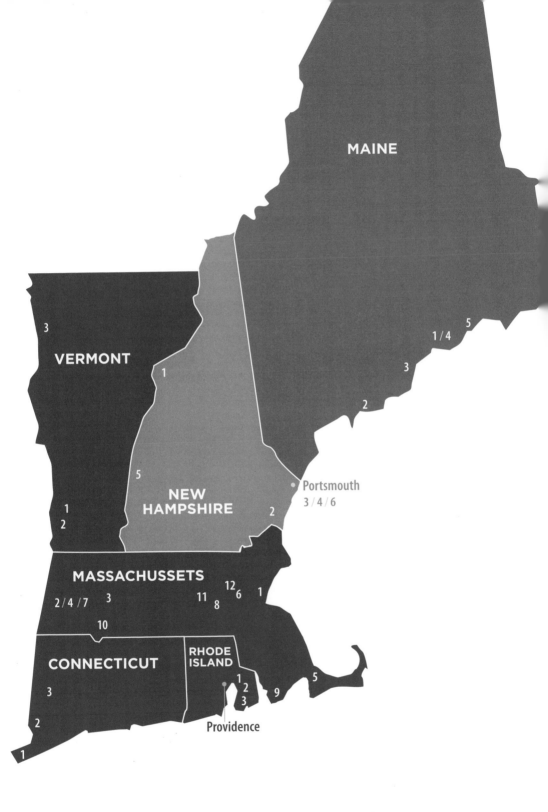

MAINE

VERMONT

3

1 / 4   5

3

2

1

NEW
HAMPSHIRE

5

2   Portsmouth
                3 / 4 / 6

1
2

MASSACHUSSETS

2 / 4 / 7   3   11   12   6   1
                                    8

10

CONNECTICUT   RHODE
                        ISLAND

3   1
                                2
2   3   9   5

1   Providence

MAINE (5)

1. Asticou Azalea Garden, Mount Desert
2. **Coastal Maine Botanical Gardens, Boothbay**
3. Merryspring Nature Center, Camden
4. Thuya Garden, Mount Desert
5. Wild Gardens of Acadia, Bar Harbor

NEW HAMPSHIRE (6)

1. **The Fells, Newbury**
2. Fuller Gardens, North Hampton
3. Moffatt-Ladd House & Garden, Portsmouth
4. Prescott Park, Portsmouth
5. **Saint-Gaudens National Historic Site, Cornish**
6. Strawbery Banke Museum, Portsmouth

VERMONT (3)

1. **Hildene, Manchester**
2. Park-McCullough, North Bennington
3. Shelburne Farms, Shelburne

CONNECTICUT (3)

1. Bartlett Arboretum & Gardens, Stamford
2. **Garden of Ideas, Ridgefield**
3. Glebe House & Gertrude Jekyll Garden, Woodbury

MASSACHUSETTS (12)

1. **Arnold Arboretum, Boston**
2. Berkshire Botanical Garden, Stockbridge
3. Botanic Garden of Smith College, Northampton
4. Chesterwood, Stockbridge
5. Heritage Museum & Gardens, Sandwich
6. Massachusetts Horticultural Society, Wellesley
7. **Naumkeag, Stockbridge**
8. New England Wild Flower Society, Framingham
9. Polly Hill Arboretum, West Tisbury
10. Stanley Park, Westfield
11. Tower Hill Botanic Garden, Boylston
12. Vale, the Lyman Estate, Waltham

RHODE ISLAND (3)

1. **Blithewold Mansion, Gardens & Arboretum, Bristol**
2. Green Animals Topiary Garden, Portsmouth
3. Newport Mansions of the Preservation Society of Newport County, Newport

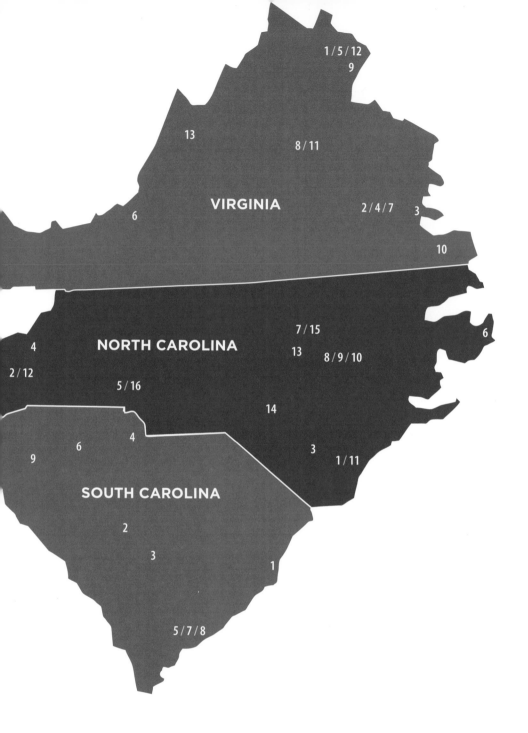

VIRGINIA

1 / 5 / 12
9
13
8 / 11
2 / 4 / 7
3
6
10

NORTH CAROLINA

7 / 15
13
8 / 9 / 10
6
4
2 / 12
5 / 16
14
3
6
4
1 / 11
9

SOUTH CAROLINA

2
3
1
5 / 7 / 8

VIRGINIA (13)

1. **Bon Air Park Rose Garden, Arlington**
2. Bryan Park Azalea Gardens, Richmond
3. Colonial Williamsburg, Williamsburg
4. **Lewis Ginter Botanical Garden, Richmond**
5. Green Spring Gardens, Alexandria
6. Hahn Horticulture Garden, Blacksburg
7. Maymont, Richmond
8. Monticello, Charlottesville
9. Mount Vernon Estate & Gardens, Mount Vernon
10. Norfolk Botanical Garden, Norfolk
11. **Pavilion Gardens, Charlottesville**
12. River Farm, Alexandria
13. Woodrow Wilson Birthplace and Gardens, Staunton

NORTH CAROLINA (16)

1. Airlie Gardens, Wilmington
2. **Biltmore Estate, Asheville**
3. Cape Fear Botanical Garden, Fayetteville
4. Daniel Boone Native Gardens, Boone
5. Daniel Stowe Botanical Garden, Belmont
6. Elizabethan Gardens, Manteo
7. Gardens of Witherspoon, Durham
8. JC Raulston Arboretum, Raleigh
9. Juniper Level Botanic Garden, Raleigh
10. Ellen Mordecai Garden, Raleigh
11. New Hanover County Co-Op Extension Arboretum, Wilmington
12. North Carolina Arboretum, Asheville
13. **North Carolina Botanical Garden, Chapel Hill**
14. Sandhills Horticultural Gardens, Pinehurst
15. **Sarah P. Duke Gardens, Durham**
16. **Wing Haven, Charlotte**

SOUTH CAROLINA (9)

1. **Brookgreen Gardens, Murrells Inlet**
2. Caldwell-Boylston Gardens/Lace House, Columbia
3. Edisto Memorial Gardens, Orangeburg
4. Glencairn Garden, Rock Hill
5. Hampton Park, Charleston
6. Hatcher Gardens & Woodland Preserve, Spartanburg
7. Magnolia Plantation and Gardens, Charleston
8. **Middleton Place, Charleston**
9. **South Carolina Botanical Garden, Clemson**

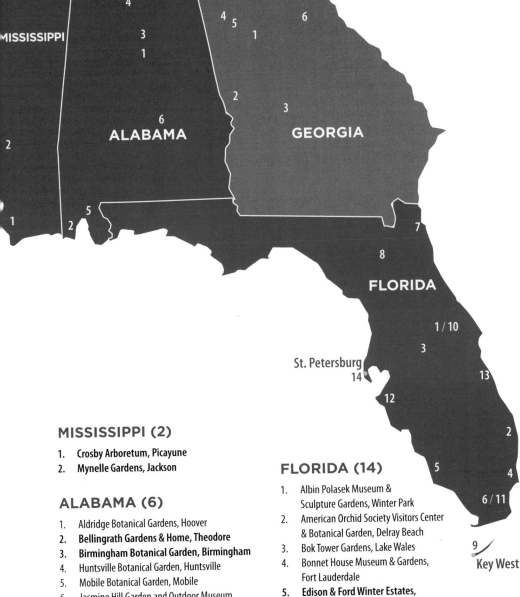

MISSISSIPPI (2)

1. **Crosby Arboretum**, Picayune
2. **Mynelle Gardens**, Jackson

ALABAMA (6)

1. Aldridge Botanical Gardens, Hoover
2. **Bellingrath Gardens & Home, Theodore**
3. **Birmingham Botanical Garden, Birmingham**
4. Huntsville Botanical Garden, Huntsville
5. Mobile Botanical Garden, Mobile
6. Jasmine Hill Garden and Outdoor Museum, Montgomery

GEORGIA (6)

1. **Atlanta Botanical Garden, Atlanta**
2. Callaway Gardens and Sibley Horticultural Center, Pine Mountain
3. Massee Lane Gardens, American Camellia Society, Fort Valley
4. Oak Hill & the Martha Berry Museum, Rome
5. Smith-Gilbert Gardens, Kennesaw
6. **State Botanical Garden of Georgia, Athens**

FLORIDA (14)

1. Albin Polasek Museum & Sculpture Gardens, Winter Park
2. American Orchid Society Visitors Center & Botanical Garden, Delray Beach
3. Bok Tower Gardens, Lake Wales
4. Bonnet House Museum & Gardens, Fort Lauderdale
5. **Edison & Ford Winter Estates, Fort Myers**
6. **Fairchild Tropical Botanic Garden, Coral Gables**
7. Jacksonville Zoo and Gardens, Jacksonville
8. Kanapaha Botanical Gardens, Gainesville
9. Key West Tropical Forest & Botanical Garden, Key West
10. **Harry P. Leu Gardens, Orlando**
11. Miami Beach Botanical Garden, Miami Beach
12. **Marie Selby Botanical Gardens, Sarasota**
13. McKee Botanical Garden, Vero Beach
14. Sunken Gardens, St. Petersburg

INDIANA (18)

1. Foellinger-Freimann Botanical Conservatory, Fort Wayne
2. Garfield Park Conservatory, Indianapolis
3. Gene Stratton-Porter State Historic Site, Rome City
4. Hayes Regional Arboretum, Richmond
5. **Hidden Hill Nursery & Sculpture Garden, Utica**
6. Hill Memorial Rose Garden, Richmond
7. Hilltop Garden & Nature Center, Bloomington
8. **Indianapolis Museum of Art, Indianapolis**
9. Lanier Mansion State Historic Site, Madison
10. Medicinal Plant Garden, Indianapolis
11. Minnetrista Center, Muncie
12. **New Harmony State Historic Site, New Harmony**
13. Purdue University Horticulture Gardens, West Lafayette
14. T.C. Steele Home State Historic Site, Nashville
15. **Taltree Arboretum & Gardens, Valparaiso**
16. Warsaw Biblical Gardens, Warsaw
17. Wellfield Botanic Gardens, Elkhart
18. White River Gardens/Indianapolis Zoo, Indianapolis

KENTUCKY (5)

1. Bernheim Arboretum and Research Forest, Clermont
2. Boone County Arboretum, Union
3. State Botanical Garden of Kentucky, Lexington
4. Western Kentucky Botanical Gardens, Owensboro
5. **Yew Dell Gardens, Crestwood**

TENNESSEE (4)

1. **Cheekwood Botanical Garden & Museum of Art, Nashville**
2. Dixon Gallery & Gardens, Memphis
3. Knoxville Botanical Garden and Arboretum, Knoxville
4. **Memphis Botanic Garden, Memphis**

ILLINOIS (10)

1. **Anderson Japanese Gardens, Rockford**
2. Cantigny, Wheaton
3. **Chicago Botanic Garden, Glencoe**
4. Garfield Park Conservatory, Chicago
5. Illinois State University Horticultural Center, Normal
6. Klehm Arboretum & Botanic Garden, Rockford
7. **Lincoln Memorial Garden & Nature Center, Springfield**
8. **Millennium Park, Chicago**
9. Morton Arboretum, Lisle
10. Quad City Botanical Garden, Rock Island

MISSOURI (5)

1. Botanical Gardens at Nathanael Greene Close Memorial Park, Springfield
2. Ewing and Muriel Kauffman Memorial Garden, Kansas City
3. **Missouri Botanical Garden, St. Louis**
4. Mizzou Botanic Garden, Columbia
5. Powell Gardens, Kingsville

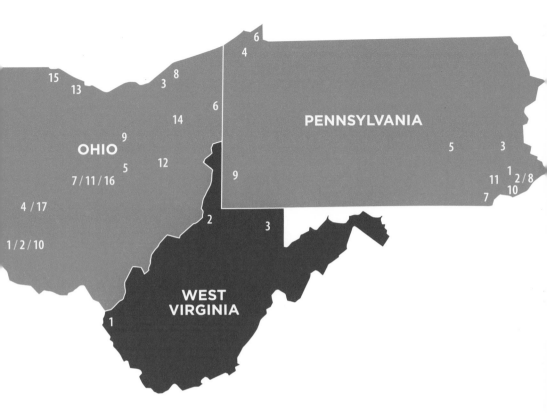

OHIO (17)

1. Cincinnati Zoo & Botanical Garden, Cincinnati
2. Civic Garden Center of Greater Cincinnati, Cincinnati
3. **Cleveland Botanical Garden, Cleveland**
4. Cox Arboretum & Gardens, Dayton
5. Dawes Arboretum, Newark
6. Fellows Riverside Gardens, Youngstown
7. **Franklin Park Conservatory, Columbus**
8. Holden Arboretum, Kirtland
9. **Kingwood Center, Mansfield**
10. Krohn Conservatory, Cincinnati
11. Ohio State University Chadwick Arboretum & Learning Center, Columbus
12. Schoepfle Garden, Birmingham
13. Schedel Arboretum & Gardens, Elmore
14. **Stan Hywet Hall & Garden, Akron**
15. Toledo Botanical Garden, Toledo
16. **Topiary Garden at Deaf School Park, Columbus**
17. Wegerzyn Gardens & Children's Discovery Garden, Dayton

PENNSYLVANIA (11)

1. **Chanticleer Garden, Wayne**
2. Bartram's Garden, Philadelphia
3. Bowman's Hill Wildflower Preserve, New Hope
4. Goodell Gardens & Homestead, Edinboro
5. Hershey Gardens, Hershey
6. Lake Erie Arboretum at Frontier Park, Erie
7. **Longwood Gardens, Kennett Square**
8. Morris Arboretum, Philadelphia
9. **Phipps Conservatory & Botanical Gardens, Pittsburgh**
10. Scott Arboretum, Swarthmore
11. Tyler Arboretum, Media

WEST VIRGINIA (3)

1. C. Fred Edwards Conservatory, Huntington
2. Prabhupada's Palace Rose Garden, Moundsville
3. **West Virginia Botanic Garden, Morgantown**

MINNESOTA (6)

1. Eloise Butler Wildflower Garden and Bird Sanctuary, Minneapolis
2. **Como Park Zoo and Marjorie McNeely Conservatory, St. Paul**
3. Linnaeus Arboretum, St. Peter
4. Living Legacy Gardens, Staples
5. Minnesota Landscape Arboretum, Chaska
6. **Munsinger Garden & Clemens Garden, St. Cloud**

IOWA (8)

1. Bickelhaupt Arboretum, Clinton
2. Brenton Arboretum, Dallas Center
3. Cedar Valley Arboretum & Botanic Gardens, Waterloo
4. Dubuque Arboretum & Botanical Gardens, Dubuque
5. Iowa Arboretum, Madrid
6. **Reiman Gardens, Ames**
7. **Seed Savers Exchange Heritage Farm, Decorah**
8. Vander Veer Botanical Park, Davenport

WISCONSIN (7)

1. Allen Centennial Gardens, Madison
2. **Boerner Botanical Garden, Hales Corners**
3. Green Bay Botanical Garden, Green Bay
4. Lyden Sculpture Garden, Milwaukee
5. Mitchell Park Conservatory, Milwaukee
6. **Olbrich Botanical Gardens, Madison**
7. **Rotary Botanical Gardens, Janesville**

MICHIGAN (17)

1. Anna Scripps Whitcomb Conservatory, Detroit
2. Cooley Gardens, Lansing
3. Cranbrook House and Gardens, Bloomfield Hills
4. Dahlia Hill, Midland
5. Dow Gardens, Midland
6. Edsel and Eleanor Ford Estate, Grosse Pointe Shores
7. **Fernwood Botanical Garden & Nature Preserve, Niles**
8. **Frederik Meijer Gardens & Sculpture Park, Grand Rapid**s
9. Grand Hotel, Mackinac Island
10. Hidden Lake Gardens, Tipton
11. Leila Arboretum Society, Battle Creek
12. Matthaei Botanical Gardens & Nichols Arboretum, Ann Arbor
13. **Michigan 4-H Children's Garden, East Lansing**
14. Michigan State Horticulture Gardens, East Lansing
15. Taylor Conservatory and Botanical Gardens, Taylor
16. Tokushima Saginaw Friendship Garden & Japanese Teahouse, Saginaw
17. Veldheer Tulip Center, Holland

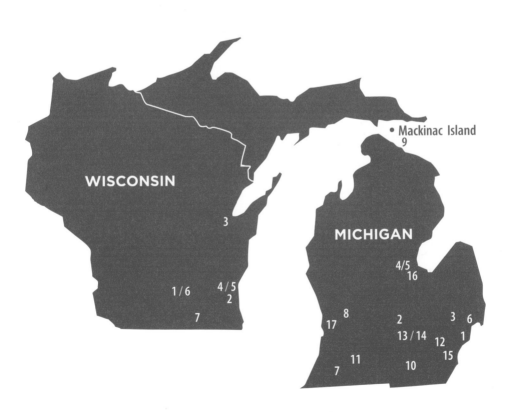

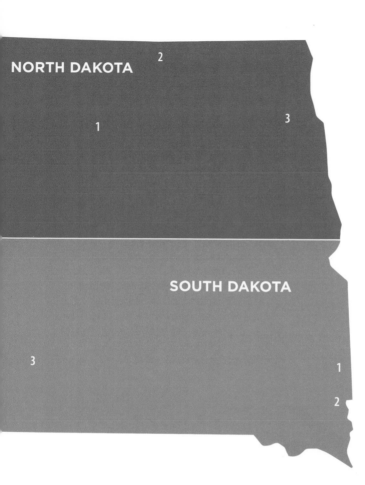

NORTH DAKOTA (3)

1. Fort Stevenson State Park Arboretum, Garrison
2. **International Peace Garden, Dunseith**
3. Myra Arboretum, Larimore

SOUTH DAKOTA (3)

1. McCrory Gardens & Arboretum, Brookings
2. **McKennan Park, Sioux Falls**
3. Memorial Park Rose Gardens, Rapid City

NEBRASKA (3)

1. Arbor Day Farm, Nebraska City
2. **Lauritzen Gardens, Omaha**
3. Joslyn Castle, Omaha

KANSAS (6)

1. **Botanica, The Wichita Gardens, Wichita**
2. **Dyck Arboretum of the Plains, Hesston**
3. Overland Park Arboretum and Botanical Garden, Overland Park
4. Reinisch Rose Garden and Doran Rock Garden, Topeka
5. Sedgwick County Extension Arboretum, Wichita
6. Ward-Meade Park Botanic Gardens, Topeka

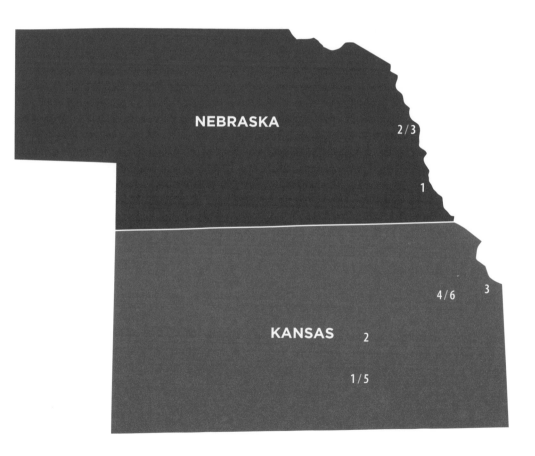

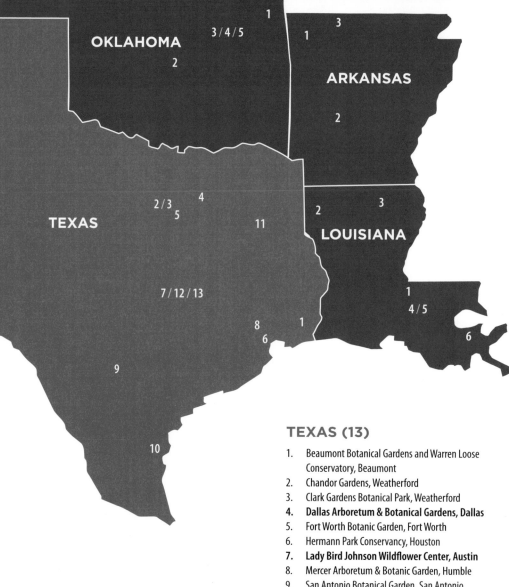

TEXAS (13)

1. Beaumont Botanical Gardens and Warren Loose Conservatory, Beaumont
2. Chandor Gardens, Weatherford
3. Clark Gardens Botanical Park, Weatherford
4. **Dallas Arboretum & Botanical Gardens, Dallas**
5. Fort Worth Botanic Garden, Fort Worth
6. Hermann Park Conservancy, Houston
7. **Lady Bird Johnson Wildflower Center, Austin**
8. Mercer Arboretum & Botanic Garden, Humble
9. San Antonio Botanical Garden, San Antonio
10. South Texas Botanical Gardens & Nature Center, Corpus Christi
11. Tyler Municipal Rose Garden, Tyler
12. Umlauf Sculpture Garden & Museum, Austin
13. **Zilker Botanical Garden, Austin**

ARKANSAS (3)

1. Botanical Garden of the Ozarks, Fayetteville
2. **Garvan Woodland Gardens, Hot Springs**
3. Eureka Springs Gardens, Eureka Springs

OKLAHOMA (5)

1. Lendonwood Gardens, Grove
2. **Myriad Botanical Gardens, Oklahoma City**
3. Oklahoma Centennial Botanical Garden, Tulsa
4. Philbrook Museum of Art, Tulsa
5. Woodward Park & Tulsa Garden Center, Tulsa

LOUISIANA (6)

1. Afton Villa and Gardens, St. Francisville
2. **American Rose Center, Shreveport**
3. Biedenharn Museum & Gardens, Monroe
4. Burden Horticulture Society, Baton Rouge
5. Hilltop Arboretum, Baton Rouge
6. **Longue Vue House & Gardens, New Orleans**

UTAH (3)

1. International Peace Gardens at Jordan Park, Salt Lake City
2. **Red Butte Garden and Arboretum, Salt Lake City**
3. Utah Botanical Center, Kaysville

COLORADO (4)

1. **Betty Ford Alpine Garden, Vail**
2. Colorado Springs Utilities Xeriscape Demonstration Garden, Colorado Springs
3. **Denver Botanic Gardens, Denver**
4. Western Colorado Botanical Gardens, Grand Junction

NEW MEXICO (4)

1. Albuquerque Rose Garden, Albuquerque
2. **Rio Grande Botanic Garden, Albuquerque**
3. **Santa Fe Botanical Garden/Leonora Curtain Wetland Preserve, Sante Fe**
4. Salman's Santa Fe Greenhouses, Santa Fe

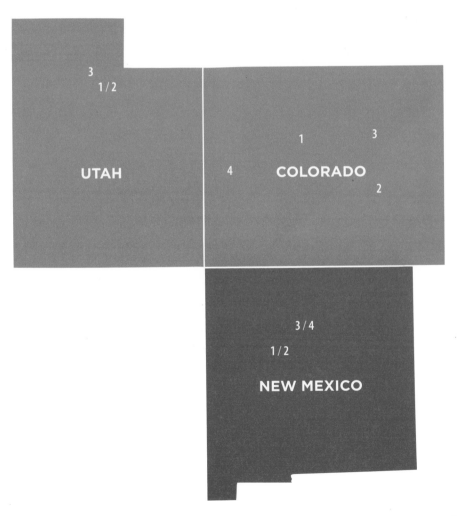

NEVADA (3)

1. Ethel M Botanical Cactus Garden, Henderson
2. **Gardens at the Springs Preserve, Las Vegas**
3. University of Nevada Las Vegas Arboretum, Las Vegas

ARIZONA (4)

1. Arboretum at Flagstaff, Flagstaff
2. **Arizona-Sonora Desert Museum, Tucson**
3. **Desert Botanical Garden, Phoenix**
4. Tucson Botanical Garden, Tucson

Seattle
3 / 11 / 12

WASHINGTON

OREGON

MONTANA

IDAHO

WYOMING

WASHINGTON (12)

1. Bellevue Botanical Garden, Bellevue
2. Bloedel Reserve, Bainbridge Island
3. **Dunn Gardens, Seattle**
4. Evergreen Arboretum and Gardens, Everett
5. Kruckeberg Botanic Garden, Shoreline
6. Lake Wilderness Arboretum, Maple Valley
7. Lakewold Gardens, Lakewood
8. Little & Lewis Water Gardens, Bainbridge Island
9. **Manito Park and Botanical Gardens, Spokane**
10. W.W. Seymour Botanical Conservatory, Tacoma
11. University of Washington Botanic Gardens, Seattle
12. University of Washington Medicinal Herb Garden, Seattle

OREGON (6)

1. Azalea Park, Brookings
2. Crystal Springs Rhododendron Garden, Portland
3. Hoyt Arboretum, Portland
4. Mount Pisgah Arboretum, Eugene
5. **Oregon Garden, Silverton**
6. **Portland Japanese Garden, Portland**

IDAHO (3)

1. **Idaho Botanical Garden, Boise**
2. Sawtooth Botanical Garden, Ketchum
3. University of Idaho Charles Houston Shattuck Arboretum & Botanical Garden, Moscow

WYOMING (1)

1. Cheyenne Botanic Gardens, Cheyenne

MONTANA (3)

1. Daly Mansion, Hamilton
2. Memorial Rose Garden, Missoula
3. **Tizer Botanic Gardens & Arboretum, Jefferson City**

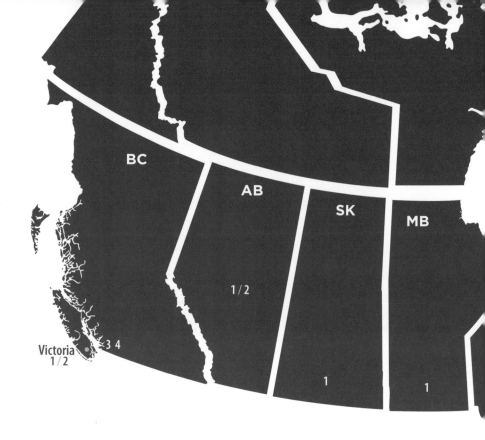

CANADA

BRITISH COLUMBIA (4)

1. **Butchart Gardens, Victoria**
2. Glendale Gardens at the Horticulture Centre of the Pacific, Victoria
3. University of British Columbia Botanic Garden, Vancouver
4. **Minter Gardens, Chilliwack**

ALBERTA (2)

1. **Devonian Botanic Garden, Edmonton**
2. Muttart Conservatory, Edmonton

SASKATCHEWAN (1)

1. Wascana Centre, Regina

MANITOBA (1)

1. Living Prairie Museum, Winnipeg

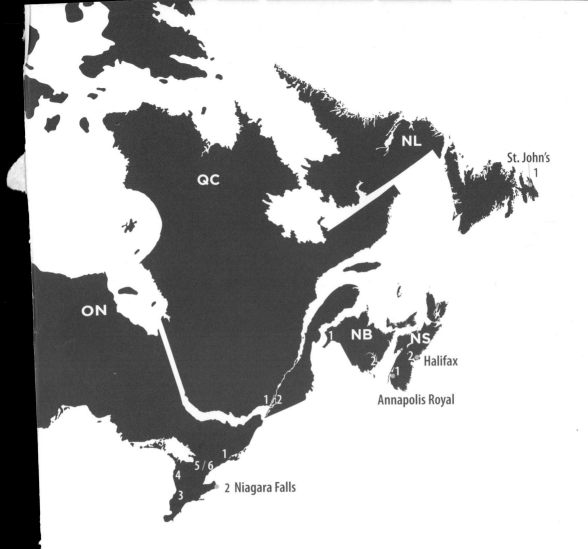

ONTARIO (6)

1. Guild Inn Sculpture Garden, Scarborough
2. **Niagara Parks Botanical Garden and School of Horticulture, Niagara Falls**
3. **Royal Botanic Gardens, Burlington**
4. Shakespearean Gardens, Stratford
5. **Spadina Historic House and Gardens, Toronto**
6. Toronto Music Garden, Toronto

QUEBEC (2)

1. **Jardins des Floralies, Montreal**
2. Montreal Botanical Garden and Insectarium, Montreal

NEW BRUNSWICK (2)

1. Horticultural Gardens Rockwood Park, Saint John
2. **New Brunswick Botanical Garden, Saint Jacques**

NEWFOUNDLAND (1)

1. Newfoundland Memorial University, St. John's

NOVA SCOTIA (2)

1. **Annapolis Royal Historic Gardens, Annapolis Royal**
2. Halifax Public Garden, Halifax

Meet Jo Ellen Meyers Sharp

Jo Ellen Meyers Sharp is a professional writer and inveterate garden visitor. She has been writing about gardens and gardening since 1989, when she began writing for *The Indianapolis Star*. In addition to maintaining a weekly gardening column for the *Star*, Sharp regularly contributes articles to *Indiana Gardening* and *Angie's List Magazine*.

Jo Ellen serves as a regional director of the Garden Writers Association, a national organization dedicated to serving the garden writing community. In addition to being an Advanced Master Gardener, Sharp is involved with her community by serving on the boards of many organizations.

This is her second book. Jo Ellen Meyers Sharp is co-author of the *Indiana Gardener's Guide* (2003), also for Cool Springs Press.

Jo Ellen has personally visited dozens of the gardens in this guide and has many more on her life list. An Indianapolis native, Sharp was born into the business as a child of German immigrants who operated greenhouses and a florist. She still lives in Indianapolis, when she's not out visiting public gardens around the country.